MACMILLA

General Editor: James Gibson

Published:

JANE AUSTEN: **PRIDE AND PRE**
    EMMA Norman Page
    MANSFIELD PARK Richard Wirdnam
ROBERT BOLT: **A MAN FOR ALL SEASONS** Leonard Smith
EMILY BRONTË: **WUTHERING HEIGHTS** Hilda D. Spear
GEOFFREY CHAUCER: **THE PROLOGUE TO THE CANTERBURY TALES**
    Nigel Thomas and Richard Swan
    THE MILLER'S TALE Michael Alexander
CHARLES DICKENS: **BLEAK HOUSE** Dennis Butts
   , **GREAT EXPECTATIONS** Dennis Butts
    HARD TIMES Norman Page
GEORGE ELIOT: **MIDDLEMARCH** Graham Handley
    SILAS MARNER Graham Handley
E. M. FORSTER: **A PASSAGE TO INDIA** Hilda D. Spear
THE METAPHYSICAL POETS Joan van Emden
WILLIAM GOLDING: **LORD OF THE FLIES** Raymond Wilson
OLIVER GOLDSMITH: **SHE STOOPS TO CONQUER** Paul Ranger
THOMAS HARDY: **FAR FROM THE MADDING CROWD** Colin Temblett-Wood
    TESS OF THE D'URBERVILLES James Gibson
CHRISTOPHER MARLOWE: **DOCTOR FAUSTUS** David A. Male
ARTHUR MILLER: **THE CRUCIBLE** Leonard Smith
GEORGE ORWELL: **ANIMAL FARM** Jean Armstrong
WILLIAM SHAKESPEARE: **MACBETH** David Elloway
    A MIDSUMMER NIGHT'S DREAM Kenneth Pickering
    ROMEO AND JULIET Helen Morris
    THE WINTER'S TALE Diana Devlin
    HENRY IV PART I Helen Morris
GEORGE BERNARD SHAW: **ST JOAN** Leonée Ormond
RICHARD SHERIDAN: **THE RIVALS** Jeremy Rowe
    THE SCHOOL FOR SCANDAL Paul Ranger

Forthcoming:

SAMUEL BECKETT: **WAITING FOR GODOT** J. Birkett
WILLIAM BLAKE: **SONGS OF INNOCENCE AND SONGS OF EXPERIENCE**
    A. Tomlinson
GEORGE ELIOT: **THE MILL ON THE FLOSS** H. Wheeler
T. S. ELIOT: **MURDER IN THE CATHEDRAL** P. Lapworth
HENRY FIELDING: **JOSEPH ANDREWS** T. Johnson
E. M. FORSTER: **HOWARD'S END** I. Milligan
WILLIAM GOLDING: **THE SPIRE** R. Sumner
THOMAS HARDY: **THE MAYOR OF CASTERBRIDGE** R. Evans
SELECTED POEMS OF GERALD MANLEY HOPKINS
PHILIP LARKIN: **THE WHITSUN WEDDING AND THE LESS DECEIVED**
    A. Swarbrick
D. H. LAWRENCE: **SONS AND LOVERS** R. Draper
HARPER LEE: **TO KILL A MOCKINGBIRD** Jean Armstrong
THOMAS MIDDLETON: **THE CHANGELING** A. Bromham
ARTHUR MILLER: **DEATH OF A SALESMAN** P. Spalding
WILLIAM SHAKESPEARE: **HAMLET** J. Brooks
    HENRY V P. Davison
    KING LEAR F. Casey
    JULIUS CAESAR David Elloway
    MEASURE FOR MEASURE M. Lilly
    OTHELLO Christopher Beddows
    RICHARD II C. Barber
    TWELFTH NIGHT Edward Leeson
    THE TEMPEST Kenneth Pickering
TWO PLAYS OF JOHN WEBSTER David A. Male

MACMILLAN MASTER GUIDES
A PASSAGE TO INDIA
BY E. M. FORSTER

HILDA D. SPEAR

MACMILLAN

First edition 1986

Published by
MACMILLAN EDUCATION LTD
Houndmills, Basingstoke, Hampshire RG21 2XS
and London
Companies and representatives
throughout the world

Typeset in Great Britain by
TecSet Ltd, Sutton, Surrey

Printed in Hong Kong

British Library Cataloguing in Publication Data
Spear, Hilda D.
A passage to India by E. M. Forster.—
(Macmillan master guides)
1. Forster, E. M. Passage to India
I. Title   II. Forster, E. M. Passage to India
823'.912   PR6011.O58P37
ISBN 0-333-39616-2 Pbk
ISBN 0-333-39617-0 Pbk export

CONTENTS

To Walter — again

GENERAL EDITOR'S PREFACE

The aim of the Macmillan Master Guides is to help you to appreciate the book you are studying by providing information about it and by suggesting ways of reading and thinking about it which will lead to a fuller understanding. The section on the writer's life and background has been designed to illustrate those aspects of the writer's life which have influenced the work, and to place it in its personal and literary context. The summaries and critical commentary are of special importance in that each brief summary of the action is followed by an examination of the significant critical points. The space which might have been given to repetitive explanatory notes has been devoted to a detailed analysis of the kind of passage which might confront you in an examination. Literary criticism is concerned with both the broader aspects of the work being studied and with its detail. The ideas which meet us in reading a great work of literature, and their relevance to us today, are an essential part of our study, and our Guides look at the thought of their subject in some detail. But just as essential is the craft with which the writer has constructed his work of art, and this may be considered under several technical headings – characterisation, language, style and stagecraft, for example.

The authors of these Guides are all teachers and writers of wide experience, and they have chosen to write about books they admire and know well in the belief that they can communicate their admiration to you. But you yourself must read and know intimately the book you are studying. No one can do that for you. You should see this book as a lamppost. Use it to shed light, not to lean against. If you know your text and know what it is saying about life, and how it says it, then you will enjoy it, and there is no better way of passing an examination in literature.

JAMES GIBSON

ACKNOWLEDGEMENTS

I should like to thank Carolyn Bain of Dundee University Geography Department for preparing the map of India, the staff of the Libraries of Dundee University and Duncan of Jordanstone College of Art for their ready assistance in various ways, Mrs Moira Anthony for help with typing and my daughter Kathryn for help with both typing and proof-reading.

HILDA D. SPEAR

The author and publishers wish to thank Edward Arnold (Publishers) Ltd for extracts from *A Passage to India* by E. M. Forster.

Cover illustration: *Celebrations in India* by M. E. Caddy, courtesy of the Bridgeman Art library.

INTRODUCTION:
ON READING A NOVEL

When we read a novel – any novel – what do we expect from it? Is our first purpose to be informed, to be educated, to receive a moral, a social or a political lesson? It should not be: novels are meant to be enjoyed – enjoy them! The very worst way to read a novel for the first time is to read with pen in hand laboriously taking notes as you go; but notice those words 'for the first time': any novel worth reading is worth reading twice – or three times – or again and again and again! No one can read a novel for you; someone may tell you the story but this is merely the skeleton, which the novelist fleshes out; the novel itself is much more than mere story. A quick first reading will help you to find your way about a novel but it will not have told you all about it. This introduction suggests some lines of thought for you to follow on your second and subsequent readings.

Who narrates the story? Is it told in the first person, the 'I' being the subject of the tale? Or is it perhaps in the third person, an omniscient narrator observing objectively the actions and thoughts of all the protagonists? Or is it more subtle than either of these simple methods? Are there several tellers, looking at the story from their own differing viewpoints, or telling different parts of the story? Is the main narrator an auditor too, who receives the story from one or more other narrators? Or is it difficult to decide who is telling the story, as it seems to be happening in the minds of the characters themselves? The method of narration has always exercised novelists, for on it depends the understanding and varying sympathies of the reader. A reminiscent first person story starts off with certain presuppositions – at least the protagonist survives and is able to tell the tale. On the other hand, the all-knowing third person narrator may predispose us to like or dislike particular characters; we may even feel that our sympathies are being manipulated.

From what point of view do we see the events of the novel? The straightforward first person narrator will tell the story from his own point of view; even if he attempts to show us other points of view they will be sifted through his own and we shall receive an essentially subjective account. The third person narration, from an impartial outside observer, generally purports to be objective; as soon as the narration is complicated, however, by the use of narrators with some sort of identity within the novel, then we must take into account narrative fallibility. The author may deliberately choose to have an unreliable or dishonest or naïve narrator; or perhaps one or more of the narrators will not have access to full information; on the other hand, a number of different subjective accounts of the same incident may give the reader an objective view. Certainly the narrative mode allows of wide variety and perhaps the only golden rule here is, 'Never confuse the narrator with the author'.

We can move on from discussion of the narrative method to consider the use of time in the novel. Even if there is no obvious exploitation of time as a narrative device we cannot avoid at least some thoughts on its significance. When was the novel written? If it was written fifty, or a hundred, or two hundred years ago we must remember the differences that scientific and technological advances have made to our lives today, the differences in cleanliness, in household convenience, in leisure activities, in travel and communication; we must remember the differences in social, moral and religious attitudes and in family life. We shall also have to come to terms with the vocabulary and the prose style of an older novel. An historical novel may compound our problems, for we may be observing events of hundreds or thousands of years ago, interpreted through the understanding of an author from an age that is already past.

There are, however, other aspects of the novelist's use of time which we need to consider as we read. The simplest of these is that we may have to cope, in a few hours' reading, with the events of many years and adjust, in minutes, our response to slowly altering circumstances and gradual changes in character. More complicated are the deliberate time-shifts which the novelist makes in order to achieve particular effects: the flashback, the flashforward, the events narrated in reverse order, the events narrated more than once and at different points in the novel. Observe these as you read and ask yourself what the author achieves by playing with time in such ways.

Then there is the question of place. Where is the action of the novel set? Is it in some distant, exotic, foreign land that most of us will never see? Is it in the country? In the town? Is it so unfamiliar that it warrants several pages of description? Or is it familiar enough to need none? How essential to the plot is the setting? Does it give atmosphere to the novel? Or is it entirely insignificant, referred to hardly at all? The sense of place may well reinforce themes within the novel, or different characters may be associated with different places, the aspects of which reflect the characters themselves.

Of course, you will think about the characters as you read their story. You will decide who is the hero (if there is a hero) and who is the heroine (if there is a heroine) and even who is the villain (if there is a villain); but how are these characters portrayed? Are they cardboard figures, lacking solidity? Are they caricatures, with only one feature of the characters emphasised? Are they mere reflectors, throwing light on other characters? Are they functional, fulfilling a particular but limited role? Or do they seem to be real people, reacting differently according to the circumstances, showing various aspects of their character, changing, growing, gaining our human sympathy and understanding? A good novel will probably have most if not all of these types of characters; those we respond to most readily are the ones who seem to be real but, as in life, there will be many characters who are seen briefly, superficially, who play their part in the plot and disappear from the scene; without them the novel would be poorer.

When Polonius asked Hamlet what he was reading, the reply was 'Words, words, words'. A novel is composed of words and ultimately its success depends on the choice of words, the use of language and the style for, skilfully couched in telling phrases, the dullest story may blossom, whilst the most exciting incidents may appear dull and insipid if they are recounted in flat tones and commonplace clichés. Observe how your author uses language. Is there a variety of style – formal? Colloquial? Poetic? Are there recurrent words and phrases? Realistic pictures which become images and symbols? Catchwords? Motifs? Repetitions? References? Quotations? Allusions? Is there dialogue? Do the characters speak in their own special idiom? Are we given the thoughts in their minds? Perhaps the very fact that we had not noticed the peculiarities of the language on a first reading demonstrates the skill of the author. However, that a technique is unobtrusive does not mean that it is insignificant and the better critics we become, the more we shall observe not only *what* is said but *how* it is said.

Perhaps the final needful question is, 'How do we become better critics?' Have courage! Many of us have asked ourselves this in our time. First, *believe in yourself*. Read the novel through quickly, then read it again more slowly, giving thought to some of the questions outlined above. Only after this stage should you turn to the critics. You may then find that some of your own ideas about the book have been corroborated and this may suggest that you are working on the right lines. You may also find that other ideas you have had are in disagreement with the critic you are reading. Accept that you may be wrong but do not be afraid to suspect that the critic may be wrong. Go back to the text; it is the final arbiter; does it appear to support your argument or the critic's argument? Never try to defend an indefensible position. If you cannot prove your contention, give in gracefully; however, if you still feel you are proved right, do not allow yourself to be bullied by the printed word. Any teacher worth

his or her salt learns a lot from students; every critic is vulnerable. Enjoy
your novel-reading and go on reading more novels. You may well find that
in the process you have yourself become a critic.

1 E. M. FORSTER:
LIFE AND BACKGROUND

E. M. Forster was born on New Year's Day 1879, in London. He was intended to be called Henry after his paternal great-grandfather (the father of Marianne Thornton, his mother's patron and his father's aunt), and was, indeed, registered as 'Henry Morgan Forster'; through an odd mistake, however, he was christened Edward after his father. It hardly mattered for throughout his life he was known by his second name, Morgan. A previous child of the marriage had died at birth and the young Forster was not yet two years old when, in October 1880, his father died of tuberculosis. Thus, the novelist was left to be brought up as the only child of his widowed mother; he was surrounded from an early age almost exclusively by female relatives – his great-aunt Marianne and her dependent niece Henrietta; his mother and his maternal grandmother Louisa Whichelo; his mother's friend Maimie, the widow of Henrietta's brother; and his mother's three younger sisters.

In 1883 Forster and his mother went to live at Rooksnest, an attractive country house near Stevenage in Hertfordshire. He came to love this house where they lived for ten years and it later served as the model for Howards End. Like so many only children left fatherless, he was constantly molly-coddled, under the mistaken impression that he might have inherited his father's weak chest. A photograph of him with his mother about this time shows him with shoulder-length curls and dressed in a velvet 'Little Lord Fauntleroy' suit with lace collar and cuffs.

As time went on, the boy, with the impatience of youth, grew more and more irritated with his very elderly great-aunt but when she died in 1887 at the age of ninety she left him a legacy of £8000 which gave him a measure of independence he could not otherwise have experienced.

Until he was eleven, in 1890, Forster was tutored at home; after that he was sent as a boarder to a small preparatory school in Eastbourne. Almost from the outset he found school uncongenial. Small, slight and in no way athletic, he was unpopular and subjected to various kinds of bullying. He was so unhappy there that it was decided when the time came, not to send him away to Public School but to send him instead as a day-boy to Tonbridge School; consequently – and partly because their lease on Rooksnest had run out – they moved to Tonbridge. The decision was little short of disastrous. Day-boys were despised and looked upon as socially inferior; additionally, Forster once more came in for a great deal of bullying and was very miserable. In *The Longest Journey* (1907) he castigates the Public School ethos and denigrates Tonbridge in the guise of Sawston School. However, he gained a sound classical education there; during his last year he won school prizes for both Latin and English and was offered a place at King's College, Cambridge, where he went in 1897.

If school had been a confining and repressive influence, Cambridge enfranchised him. He read widely, attended lectures assiduously and at the same time developed his interest in music and art. He now found himself in the company of a number of like-minded young men with whom he could discuss literature, philosophy or any other subject that took their fancy. In the intellectual ferment of this time he abjured Christianity, though he never lost his interest in religion in its widest sense. After three years he gained an Upper Second in his Classical Tripos and stayed on at King's for a further year to read History, again achieving no more than a Second Class. During this year he was elected to the 'Apostles', that celebrated Cambridge Society to which have belonged so many of the famous and notorious.

In his first long vacation from Cambridge he and his mother had moved house from Tonbridge to nearby Tunbridge Wells. Though Sawston School in *The Longest Journey* is essentially Tonbridge, Sawston itself is undoubtedly Tunbridge Wells and through the character of Caroline Abbott in *Where Angels Fear to Tread* Forster censures its 'idleness. . .stupidity. . . respectability [and] petty unselfishness'.

After Cambridge, Forster toyed for a while with the idea of becoming a schoolmaster but decided, with some of the money he had inherited from Marianne Thornton, to travel on the Continent. He had already tried his hand at writing and had published essays in various University magazines; he now thought that travel would perhaps further his ambitions in this line. Thus, in October 1901, he started with his mother for Italy. They were away for almost a year, spending most of the time in Italy but visiting Sicily briefly and ending up in the Austrian Tyrol. Back at home, Forster considered finding employment but did little beyond taking a weekly class in Latin at the Working Men's College in Bloomsbury. The following spring he decided to go on his travels again and he set out with his mother for Italy once more; this time he left her in Florence whilst he went on a Greek cruise.

His post-Cambridge travels seemed to give him the stimulus he needed for concentrated creativity. They provided him with a background to contrast with his restricted and restricting life in suburban England; they gave him insights into characters that he had not met with before and they realised for him the link between the romance of the unknown and the widening of horizons that he had experienced at Cambridge. He began to work on, but was unable at that time to finish, a 'Lucy' novel which was the way Forster described the then untitled novel that became eventually *A Room With a View* (1908). During his Greek trip he gestated a number of short stories which were later published in *The Celestial Omnibus* (1911) and on his return from his second journey, in late summer 1904, he began *Where Angels Fear To Tread* (1905). Simultaneously, he was extending his activities in other fields: he was commissioned to edit Virgil's *Aeneid* for Dent's classics and he offered a series of extra-mural lectures on various aspects of Italian history and culture. Yet his thirst for foreign travel was not assuaged and he accepted an invitation to go for a few months as tutor to the daughters of Countess Von Arnim, an ex-patriate Englishwoman living in a vast, old country house or *Schloss* in Germany. (She was a minor novelist and well-known at the time as author of *Elizabeth And Her German Garden* (1898)).

Where Angels Fear To Tread was published in 1905 but already the next two novels were being planned and written. Creatively, Forster was going through a period of intense activity. In his personal life, however, he was far from happy. He had by now come to understand his homosexual proclivities and though he had probably not experienced sexual consummation he had fairly certainly felt erotic impulses in the company of various of his friends and, particularly with H. O. Meredith, one of his Cambridge acquaintances, it seems likely that he had enjoyed physical caresses. It was at this point of his life that he was introduced as Latin tutor to the young Moslem Indian, Syed Ross Masood, who was preparing to go up to Oxford. A strikingly handsome young man, Masood was also lively and intelligent; Forster found himself immediately drawn to him and, before long, hopelessly in love – hopelessly, because Masood did not share his homosexual tendencies. Nevertheless, their encounter was very rewarding for the novelist, opening out new vistas for him and bringing him into close contact with an impulsive and demonstrative personality who valued friendship highly and put personal relationships first.

In April 1907 *The Longest Journey* was published. Technically a less perfect novel than the previous one, it was reviewed more harshly, yet Forster always had a special affection for this book. It is the most autobiographical of all his novels, reflecting not so much actual incidents, but rather aspects of his imaginative and spiritual life. *A Room With A View* came out in 1908 and was followed in 1910 by *Howards End* and in 1911 by the collection of short stories *The Celestial Omnibus*. It was the end of a six-year period of intense creative activity. The following year he started a new novel, *Arctic Summer*, which, despite the considerable efforts he put into it for a while, was eventually abandoned. He tried his hand at writing plays but, though he completed several, even he himself realised that they were unsatisfactory and they did not get as far as publication.

Then the opportunity arose for a journey to India and in October 1912, in the company of some friends, he set out for Bombay. There he parted from his friends and went to stay with Masood for a while before travelling about the country. During this visit to India he saw both Anglo-India and native states; he went to Bankipore and visited the Barabar Hills and Caves. He also stayed briefly in two native states, Chhatarpur and Dewas Senior. Certainly he returned home with many impressions and experiences which were later to find their way into *A Passage to India* but he was not yet ready to write the novel. Instead, an almost chance encounter led him to write *Maurice*. This book, unlike his other novels, over all of which he struggled and agonised, sprang into his mind almost complete in its conception: 'The general plan,' he wrote in 1960, 'the three characters, the happy ending for two of them, all rushed into my pen. And the whole thing went through without a hitch' (published in a 'Terminal Note' to the first edition, 1971). The novel was written in record time and, having written it, Forster realised that it could not be published, for the social climate of the time was hostile to homosexuality.

Since his return from India he had gradually become involved with the Bloomsbury Group of writers and artists. He already liked and admired Leonard Woolf and soon counted Virginia Woolf among his friends. When war was declared in August 1914, with so many young men rushing to enlist, Forster decided to look for a job and he became a part-time cataloguer in the National Gallery. He was a pacifist by inclination and most of his Bloomsbury acquaintances were against the war. He was already thirty-five years old, rather above the age of general enlistment; however, in 1915 he began to consider a more active role and in November he went to Egypt with the International Red Cross. He remained in Alexandria until after the Armistice, returning home in January 1919.

He now turned to journalism and in 1920 he briefly held the post of literary editor of the *Daily Herald*. The 'Indian novel' did not progress and it began to look as though his creative energy had been dissipated. It was at this point, early in 1921, that he was invited to return to the state of Dewas Senior to act as the Maharajah's secretary for a few months. After his official duties were ended he remained in India for a further two months before taking his passage home in January 1922. He still felt dispirited and unable to continue with his novel but, with encouragement from his friends, it began slowly to take shape. *A Passage To India* was eventually published in June 1924.

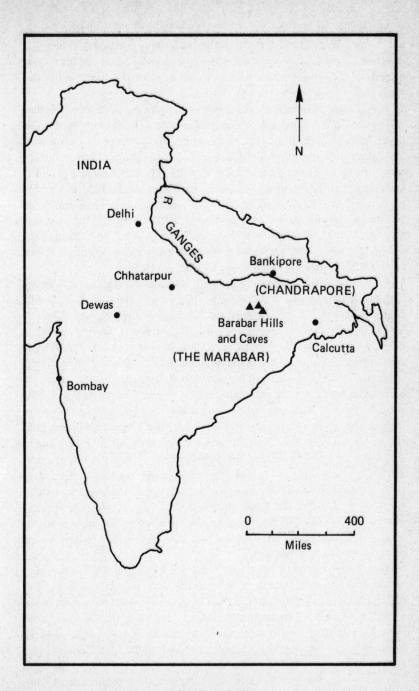

N

INDIA

Delhi

R. GANGES

Bankipore

(CHANDRAPORE)

Chhatarpur

Dewas

Barabar Hills
and Caves

(THE MARABAR)

Calcutta

Bombay

0   400

Miles

Forster's India

Meanwhile, in May of that year his Aunt Laura died and left to Forster her house, West Hackhurst, in Abinger, Surrey, which his father had designed for her. After a few months of indecision Forster and his mother moved to the house, which he was to occupy for the next twenty-two years and in which his mother was to die.

It was soon obvious from the reviews and from the sales both in Britain and in the United States that *A Passage To India* was a success, but Forster never seemed to find success encouraging. He continued to do a little journalism, to write a few short stories and some criticism but he did not settle down to any extensive creative work. He was invited by Trinity College, Cambridge to give the annual Clark Lectures in 1927 and proved to be an exceedingly popular lecturer who attracted large audiences. Following this, he was offered a three-year fellowship at King's College; this he accepted, making the proviso that he would not be resident in the college for more than six weeks a year. His eight lectures were published later in 1927 under the title *Aspects Of The Novel*.

Forster was now continually lionised; he became a regular broadcaster; a seasoned traveller, he accompanied various friends to Africa, the Middle East and eastern Europe. He enlarged his circle of literary acquaintances: he had already formed friendships with Virginia Woolf, Siegfried Sassoon, D. H. Lawrence and T. E. Lawrence; now he got to know many other contemporary writers, among them Somerset Maugham, Herbert Read, William Plomer and Christopher Isherwood. He also became active in public life: he joined the International P.E.N. (Association of Poets, Playwrights, Editors, Essayists and Novelists) club and became the first president of the young P.E.N.; in 1934 he was invited to become President of the newly founded N.C.C.L. (National Council for Civil Liberties) and in the following year he headed the British delegation to the International Writers' Congress in Paris. Back home in Abinger he was persuaded to write the spoken words and programme notes for a local pageant in aid of the Church Preservation Fund (published as the last piece in *Abinger Harvest*, 1936); Dr Ralph Vaughan Williams wrote the accompanying music; it is not many local efforts that can draw on the contributions of two such distinguished men.

During the period leading up to the Second World War Forster was involved in politics, though only from the sidelines – essays to journals such as the *New Statesman* and *Nation*, letters to national papers, some regular broadcasting; he produced little original, imaginative work, however. Already sixty at the outbreak of the war he was no longer expected to do any active war service, though he served on the local Refugee Committee. In March 1945 his mother died and Forster for the first time in his life was alone. Six months or so later the local landowner, Lord Farrer, decided to reclaim West Hackhurst, the lease of which had run out some years before. The loss of his house so soon after the death of his mother was a sore blow to Forster but just at this moment he was offered an Honorary Fellowship at King's College and was invited to take up residence there; he did so in November 1946.

He now began writing again. He spent several years on the libretto of Benjamin Britten's *Billy Budd* (first performed in December 1951); he collected together a number of essays and reviews and published them in *Two Cheers For Democracy* (1951); he wrote *The Hill Of Devi* (1953), a memoir of his visit to Dewas and *Marianne Thornton*, a biography of his great-aunt. He was accorded civic honours, being made a Companion of Honour in 1952 and awarded the Order of Merit in 1969. In the 1960s, however, his health began to fail. He died on 7 June 1970 at the age of ninety-one.

During the nineteenth century, British influence in India had been extended over the greater part of the subcontinent so that by the beginning of this century most of the country was either directly under British control (British India) or under British protection; only Nepal and the tiny state of Bhotan, both in the north-east, were independent. Forster's first journey to India in 1912 was primarily to visit his friend and ex-pupil, Syed Ross Masood, then working as a barrister in Patna, a town situated in the Bengal Plains to the north and west of Calcutta; adjoining Patna was the Anglo-Indian town of Bankipore, geographically the original of the Chandrapore of his novel. He moved on from British India to the native states of Chhatarpur and Dewas Senior which served jointly as his models for Mau. Then, before returning home, he visited the Barabar Caves, the Marabar of the novel's central section.

He had thus on his first visit collected together the principal physical features of the country which he was to use in *A Passage To India*. A novelist who constantly made use of his own experiences in his work, he had also, consciously or subconsciously, absorbed much of the other material he was to use later and had met many of the characters who, in one way or another, were to contribute to his plot. Though he began the novel, however, it did not progress.

The war intervened before Forster's second journey to India in 1921. He had spent just a week in Dewas on his previous visit, during which time he had developed a great liking for the young Rajah. Now he was invited back, ostensibly to act as secretary to the ruler who had meanwhile been elevated to the rank of Maharajah. Forster's duties were, in fact, very haphazard and uncertain and he found this aspect of his stay rather disturbing, though he was happy at the friendship which grew between him and the Maharajah. The highlight of his visit was the festival of Gokul Ashtami, the celebration which culminates in the birth of Krishna. He gives a factual account of this festival in *The Hill Of Devi*; it is dramatically reproduced in the last section of *A Passage To India* and was, perhaps, for Forster the final link in the chain of creation. When he returned to England he was at last able to write his 'Indian novel' which had been so long delayed. Yet it was not the same novel which he had embarked on almost ten years before; 'When I began the book I thought of it as a little bridge of sympathy between the East and West, but this conception has had to go, my sense of truth forbids anything so comfortable,' he wrote to Masood on 27 September 1922 (see Furbank, page 106). So the novel stands – truthful, but perhaps uncomfortable.

2 SUMMARIES AND CRITICAL COMMENTARY

2.1 PART I – MOSQUE

Chapter 1

Summary and commentary
This first chapter not only sets the scene for the novel but also prepares the themes, motifs and linguistic devices, the contrasts and hidden antagonisms to be found in India.

Here in Chandrapore, the Ganges which flows beside the city is not holy; the Indian settlement, low in the valley, is mean and sordid, the inhabitants neglected and degraded. The railway runs parallel with the river and high on the hill beyond is the British Civil Station whence the prospect is of a land, sumptuous and splendid. The sprawling, spawning disorder of the native town is contrasted with the sterile order established by the Anglo-Indian (the term used in Forster's day for the English government officials in India) community; yet, even geographically, the English look down upon the Indians.

The negative aspect of the opening: 'nothing...no bathing-steps... not to be holy here...no river front...' prepares us for the theme of emptiness and nothingness, for the ultimate failure in love and friendship which the book presents; the final paragraphs likewise prepare us, by use of such words as 'overarching...dome...circumference...vault', for the roundness and circularity which is vital to the imagery and, by use of the repeated word 'distance', for the echo image which is predominant. Already, even in this short chapter, Forster uses technique to emphasise ideas and imagery, the chapter ending where it began, with the 'extraordinary' Marabar Caves.

Chapter 2

Summary

Aziz and Mahmoud Ali have been invited to spend a social evening with their friend Hamidullah. When Aziz arrives the other two are arguing as to whether it is possible to be friends with the English. Hamidullah, who has been to university in England, thinks it is, but Mahmoud Ali disagrees; both, however, believe that when an Englishman or woman has been in India for a while his or her behaviour towards the Indians deteriorates.

Dinner is, of course, late but when it is announced no one takes any notice; first Aziz and then Mahmoud Ali wander away; then Aziz is taken to visit Hamidullah's wife, who is a distant relation of his, behind the purdah. When they finally sit down for dinner Mahmoud Ali has gone off somewhere in his carriage and has left a message that they should not wait for him. During the meal Aziz, who is a doctor, is sent for by his superior, Mr Callendar, the Civil Surgeon. He leaves Hamidullah's house reluctantly, riding on his bicycle; when his tyre goes down he completes the journey riding in a tonga (a light two-wheeled carriage pulled along by a man). He arrives at the Civil Surgeon's bungalow only to learn that Callendar has gone out and left no message. Whilst he ponders on what to do next, Mrs Callendar emerges from the bungalow together with Mrs Lesley and, ignoring Azis, they appropriate his tonga.

Irritated, Aziz leaves on foot and after a short walk he goes into a mosque to rest. He sits down and whilst he daydreams he becomes aware of an Englishwoman walking through the mosque. Erroneously assuming that she has not taken off her shoes, he shouts at her angrily. When he realises his mistake he is very sorry for his ill manners and apologises; the woman introduces herself as Mrs Moore, explaining that she has come from the Club where they are performing *Cousin Kate*. At the entrance to the mosque they sit down side by side to put on their shoes and are very quickly on friendly terms. Aziz learns that Mrs Moore's son is Ronny Heaslop, the City Magistrate, that his father is dead, that Mrs Moore has married a second time and that she has two other children, Ralph and Stella. Aziz is strangely moved, for he too has two sons and a daughter: Ahmed, Karim and Jamila. Mrs Moore's sympathy and understanding move him to talk of his grievances and, having unburdened himself, he feels happy; he escorts her as far as the Chandrapore Club and goes on his way.

Commentary

In this chapter we are introduced to the principal Indian character and to the most sympathetic of the English people in the book; the encounter between the two has been skilfully positioned in the narrative after the

Indians' discussion of the relationship between Indian and English and after the snubs delivered to Dr Aziz by Mr Callendar and his wife. Aziz's words to Mrs Moore, '. . .you are an Oriental' are echoed later in the book; here they indicate the sympathy that has so swiftly arisen between the two. Mrs Moore's comment in the mosque that 'God is here' is the first of the specific religious references in the novel and it too is repeatedly picked up in later pages. You should also notice the reference to cow-dung and to snakes, for both prove to be significant as the novel proceeds.

Forster suggests the 'muddle' of India by the disorder in Hamidullah's household: dinner is late; the guests wander away when it is ready; one of them disappears completely; yet despite this, and despite their differing opinions, there is a sense of friendliness and accord.

Chapter 3

Summary

When Mrs Moore returns to the Club *Cousin Kate* is nearly finished. Instead of rejoining the audience she goes into the billiard-room; there she is met by her travelling companion, Adela Quested, who remarks that she wants 'to see the *real* India'. Adela has come out to India to get to know Ronny better with a view to marriage. Whilst they wait for the play to finish and Ronny to come to them the Collector (Senior District Officer), Mr Turton, tells them that Ronny is dignified, which surprises his mother and worries Adela.

At the end of the play the audience pour out. Adela repeats to Ronny her desire to see the real India and is told by Mr Fielding, Principal of the Government College, to try seeing Indians; this suggestion shocks the other ladies present but Mr Turton offers to arrange a 'Bridge Party', a garden party designed to bridge the gulf between East and West.

As they go home Mrs Moore tells her son of her adventure in the mosque. Ronny does not at first realise that the young man she met was Indian; when he discovers that it was Aziz he cross-questions her carefully, remarking that he will have to report the whole matter to Major Callendar. Mrs Moore is distressed at this suggestion and before they part for the night she makes him promise not to do so. Going to hang up her coat, she finds a small wasp clinging to the peg; she does not disturb it and her words, 'Pretty dear', show an acceptance of the wasp's place in the order of things, which we come to realise is typical of Mrs Moore.

Commentary

Tension between English and Indian seen in the previous chapter from the Indian side is now shown from the other side; the Englishwomen in particular show prejudice against the Indians, which should remind us of Hamidullah's remark in the previous chapter that the English were all alike – the men after two years in India, the women after six months.

Mrs Moore's religious ideas are again introduced as she quietly taunts Mrs Callendar with the idea that dead natives might go to heaven. This idea is picked up at the end of the next chapter, as too are the references to the wasp and jackals; we should remember Mrs Moore's ability to comprehend the wasp in her love; it is part of her own individual brand of universal tolerance.

Chapter 4

Summary
The Bridge Party is arranged for the following Tuesday and invitations are sent out to most of the wealthy, educated or socially acceptable Indians to come to the garden of the Club that evening. The Indians are at first suspicious of this gesture but when the Nawab Bahadur, the richest and most influential of the local Indian community, decides to accept the invitation, many of the others express their intention of doing the same. Forster emphasises, however, that those invited to the Bridge Party are but a small percentage of the Indian people; using his echo image he suggests the countless millions who are beyond the remotest possibility of invitations.

This short chapter ends with a comment on the two local missionaries, old Mr Graysford and young Mr Sorley. Not members of the Club, their religion encourages them to teach universal brotherhood: God's heavenly house is open to black and white as long as they go to him in love. Nevertheless, the two men disagree about the extent of God's love, for Mr Graysford believes that animals have no part in heaven, whilst Mr Sorley will allow the possibility of monkeys and jackals, even all mammals, being accepted, but draws the line at wasps, plant life and lower forms of being.

Commentary
It is impossible for a summary to do justice to this novel, for its texture is very dense. Here in this chapter very little happens yet Forster has told us about purdah, has shown the Indians divided against themselves, but responding to a leader from their own ranks; we see that Indians may be wealthy, owning cars and having more than enough money, yet there may well be others naked, primitive and completely outside our comprehension.

The last paragraph picks up a number of earlier references: Mrs Moore's comment that 'God is love' and her discussion with the Club women about heaven and missionaries; the wasp and jackals referred to at the end of the previous chapter.

Chapter 5

Summary
The Bridge Party takes place but, far from bridging the gulf between East and West, it accentuates it. Every Indian present is suspected of ulterior motives and one mismanages his horse so that he drives his carriage over and ruins a flower bed in the club garden. Among the Anglo-Indians only Mr Turton, Mr McBryde and Mr Fielding make any real effort to talk to their Indian guests; Mrs Moore and Adela try to find a point of contact but because of the general attitude of the Club women they are not very successful. However, two invitations result from the Bridge Party, both of which suggest further possibilities of establishing friendly relations with the Indians; the first is an invitation to the home of Mr and Mrs Bhattacharya; the second is to a tea party at Government College to meet Professor Godbole and Dr Aziz.

After the Bridge Party Mrs Moore, Adela and Ronny entertain Miss Derek and the McBrydes to dinner, eating a typical, badly-prepared, expatriate menu. When their guests have departed and Adela gone to bed Ronny talks to his mother about India; the hard-headed, unsympathetic tone of his comments distresses her and she tells him that his attitude is wrong. The burden of her remarks to him is that God is love and that love is the most significant of all relationships, even in India. The conversation over, however, she reflects that, since coming to India, she has found God less and less of a comfort for she senses an emptiness, a nullity beyond the furthest echoes of human imagination.

Commentary
Here we see the first and official attempt to establish personal relationships between the British and the Indians; formally imposed from above it was doomed to failure. The echo image, beginning with the kites hovering overhead, establishes the sense of unease, itself echoed in Mrs Turton's comments about superiority. Before the chapter ends a second attempt to bridge the gap has been put in hand; though the visit to the Bhattacharyas proves to be a non-starter, there seems to be some hope in Mr Fielding's planned tea party.

Chapter 6

Summary
When he hears of the Bridge Party, Aziz agrees to go to it with his colleague, Dr Panna Lal, in the latter's new dogcart. The day itself, however, turns out to be the anniversary of the death of Aziz's wife and he determines not to go. He thinks of his marriage and his three children and

remembers that he began to love his wife only shortly before her death. He decides to send his children a telegram and goes to the post office; in the meantime, Dr Panna Lal has arrived and gone away again. Aziz now takes his wife's photograph out of a locked drawer and wallows for a while in sentimental emotion. Then he locks it away again and goes to visit Hamidullah, only to be told that his friend is at the Bridge Party. Aziz borrows Hamidullah's pony and polo equipment and goes to the Maidan (parade-ground) to knock the ball about. He is joined in a makeshift game by a young subaltern and for a brief time there is perfect accord between the two.

They part as the Bridge Party is breaking up and Aziz is confronted by Dr Panna Lal who is annoyed and irritated; not only had Aziz let him down but also his horse had got out of control and ruined some of the flowers in the Club garden. A quarrel ensues and on a sudden impulse Aziz gallops close to the dog-cart and Dr Lal's horse bolts. It is only later that Aziz wonders whether it was wise to make an enemy of his colleague and to shun the Collector's Bridge Party. When he arrives home Mr Fielding's invitation to tea is awaiting him.

Commentary

This chapter runs chronologically parallel to the previous one. There we had witnessed Dr Panna Lal's accident; now we learn his name and that Aziz had promised to help him manage his horse; thus this little incident is drawn more closely into the plot. Simultaneously, Forster shows that there are divisions between the Indians themselves, whilst a similarity of interest can at least for a while establish a friendly relationship between an Indian and an Englishman.

Aziz's thoughts about his wife's death are part of a continuing dialogue throughout the novel on the idea of heaven or afterlife and the influence of the dead upon the living.

Chapter 7

Summary

This chapter begins by telling the reader a little about Mr Fielding in order to prepare us for the account of his tea party at Government College which follows. Aziz arrives early before Fielding is dressed and the two are quickly on friendly terms; when Fielding treads on his back collar stud Aziz gives him his own, pretending it is a spare one. Adela and Mrs Moore arrive and tell Aziz and Fielding about their disappointment that morning: the Bhattacharyas had failed to send a carriage to pick them up so they had waited in vain. Aziz suggests that this is because the Bhattacharyas are Hindus and, on the spur of the moment, he invites the two ladies to visit his home. When they accept he is horrified; his bungalow is a small, shabby, sordid place, infested with flies.

When Professor Godbole arrives they have tea, the Professor who is a Deccani Brahman (or member of the priestly caste), sitting a little apart from them. Mrs Moore asks to be shown over the College and Fielding goes away with her, leaving Adela with his other two visitors. During the ensuing conversation Godbole promises to send the two ladies some sweets and, not to be outdone, Aziz suddenly invites them to the Marabar Caves. It soon becomes apparent that he knows nothing about the caves and that, though Godbole appears to know more, he will not divulge it. Suddenly Ronny appears; he is manifestly annoyed to find Adela sitting smoking with the two Indians. He and Aziz display a covert antagonism towards each other and Adela is troubled but does not know how to respond. As soon as Fielding returns, Ronny expresses his irritation and insists on taking his mother and Adela away. Before they go Godbole sings a religious song which ends on a note of nullity; though he sings 'Come, come, come, come, come, come', the god 'neglects to come'.

Commentary

The tea party is the second organised attempt to establish relationships between East and West. More personal and more informal, it appears to go well until Ronny arrives; then it breaks up and the opportunity for friendship is again lost. Once more, however, hope for connection is held out through Aziz's invitation to the Marabar Caves. We should notice here how the words 'Marabar Caves' are echoed several times and the 'extraordinary' of the first chapter is recalled.

The novel has already touched on Christianity and Mohammedanism; now the Hindu religion is presented through Godbole's song. But, like Mrs Moore's echoes and Aziz's uncertainty about an afterlife, there is a sense of emptiness at its heart: the god refuses to come. The words of Godbole's song are themselves echoed on various occasions later in the novel.

Chapter 8

Summary

On the way back to the bungalow Adela tells Mrs Moore that Aziz has invited them to the Marabar Caves. Ronny expresses annoyance at this and a quarrel ensues. After dropping Mrs Moore at the bungalow the two young people go to the Maidan to watch polo and there Adela tells Ronny that she does not wish to marry him. The actual stating of her decision somehow draws them closer together and when the Nawab Bahadur approaches with the suggestion that he should take them for a ride in his car they accept.

Ronny tells the chauffeur to take, not the Gangavati road, as the Nawab Bahadur had instructed, but the Marabar road. Night comes on and suddenly they are involved in an accident. Adela explains that she saw a large animal rush straight into the car. The Nawab Bahadur is disproportionately ruffled over the affair since no one is hurt; Ronny sees his behaviour as evidence of the unreliability of the Indian. Whilst they are waiting for the chauffeur to mend the car Miss Derek arrives, having stolen her Maharajah's car for the period of her leave; she takes Ronny, Adela and the Nawab Bahadur back to Chandrapore. Adela and Ronny now patch up their quarrel and agree to get engaged. Later, when they tell Mrs Moore of the accident, she mutters the words, 'A ghost!' After Ronny has left to do some work Adela asks Mrs Moore why she said this, but receives no satisfactory reply.

The paragraph which follows, however, moves into the Indian world and we learn that nine years previously the Nawab Bahadur had run over and killed a drunken man on the Marabar road. Though he was exonerated of blame, he had always felt that the man, in various horrific guises, lay in wait for him near the scene of his death.

The chapter ends with the threat of the approaching hot weather.

Commentary

The mystery of life in India is emphasised here by the car accident: only Adela has seen the animal that causes it; she cannot identify the animal but she suggests the possibility of a hyena. Though we are not aware of the fact until later in the chapter, the Nawab Bahadur believes it to be the spirit of the man he killed in the shape of a 'savage pig'; yet, somehow, Mrs Moore immediately refers to it as a ghost.

We see, too, how easily misunderstandings arise between East and West. Ronny harps on about Aziz forgetting his back collar stud, not realising that he had given it to Fielding in a typically generous and kindly gesture. Likewise, the young English couple cannot understand the Nawab Bahadur's reaction to the accident since they are unaware of the death on the Marabar road nine years before.

Chapter 9

Summary

Aziz is taken ill; as he lies in his bed he realises how filthy and untidy his room is; he calls on his servant, Hassan, to clear it up but nothing is done. A group of Aziz's friends come to visit him – Hamidullah, Mr Haq, Syed Mohammed and his nephew, Rafi. Almost immediately Rafi tells the others that Professor Godbole too is ill and he hints that Fielding may have poisoned both Aziz and Godbole at the party. When he says that Godbole has diarrhoea the older men cease to be suspicious of Fielding and entertain the much greater fear that this may be the beginning of a cholera epidemic. The conversation about Hindus which follows underlines the many rifts in Indian society.

Before his friends prepare to leave, Aziz recites a poem. After this Dr Panna Lal arrives with Ram Chand; he has been sent by Major Callendar to check that Aziz is really ill. He confirms that the patient has a high temperature and, when asked about Godbole, explains that there is no question of cholera; the old man is suffering from haemorrhoids. During the confused criticism of Rafi which follows, Fielding suddenly arrives. Aziz is dismayed that the Englishman should see his room still dirty and uncared-for and filled with quarrelling Indians. Hamidullah tries to calm the situation but in answer to one of his questions Fielding remarks that he does not believe in God; this immediately starts a political wrangle as to whether the English should be in India at all. After a short while the mixed company – four Mohammedans, two Hindus and an Englishman – leave together. The Indians drive away in their various conveyances and Fielding is left standing on the verandah steps as no one has bothered to fetch his horse.

Commentary

Though we are shown here informal connections being made we are aware of the deep antagonisms below the surface – the criticism of Hindus by the Mohammedans, the more subtly introduced divisions caused by the lack of a national language, Rafi's slanderous comments about Fielding's tea party, Ram Chand's general ill-will.

The interest in religion is maintained, not only through Fielding's rejection of God but through the discussion of Hindu festivals (notice again the reference to cow-dung!) and through the poem which Aziz recites, itself recalling Godbole's song to Krishna in the voiced 'need for the Friend who never comes'.

Chapter 10

Summary and commentary

Aziz's visitors find that the heat has grown even more intolerable whilst they were inside his bungalow. They disperse, feeling physically uncomfortable as the palpable heat pushes against their flesh, pricks their eyelids and pours sweat down their faces. Forster uses this chapter to prepare us for the coming hot season. It underlines the strangeness of India for the European; the bird and animal inhabitants are not only different, they impinge more upon the consciousness, for they are in constant proximity, making their own living quarters among the habitations of human kind. Furthermore, the sun is seen as unattractive, 'with power but without beauty' and the coming of the hot weather is viewed with horror.

Chapter 11

Summary
Fielding stands indecisively on the verandah for a moment and then sets off to fetch his own horse. He is arrested by a call from Aziz and he returns into the house. Quite suddenly Aziz shows him a photograph of his wife; Fielding is touched by the tremendous compliment which has been paid to him, for it is as though she has been brought out of purdah to meet him. When he puts the photograph away again Aziz explains that he has now disclosed his only secret. Fielding reflects that he has few secrets in his life but he goes on to tell Aziz that he had once, fifteen years previously, been engaged but the woman had broken it off. Aziz finds it difficult to understand that Fielding does not care to have children and does not mind that his name will die out. He proposes that Fielding should marry Adela Quested but the suggestion is swiftly rejected; he is told that anyway she is to marry Ronny Heaslop.

In the ensuing conversation Fielding displays the simplicity of his nature whilst Aziz shows the complications of the oriental character. As Fielding is about to leave, Aziz asks him to come to the Indians if he is ever in trouble but the schoolmaster does not really understand Aziz's anxiety.

Commentary
This last chapter in the first section appears to offer hopes of friendship and understanding. Fielding and Aziz show trust and affection for each other in a very light-hearted and informal way. However, we should not forget the threat of the impending hot weather, introduced in the previous chapter.

2.2 PART II – CAVES

Chapter 12

Summary and commentary
The first chapter of Part II does not forward the plot at all but it sets the scene, atmosphere and tone for the episode in the caves. The extreme antiquity of the Marabar Hills is emphasised and a sense of strangeness is evoked through the description of the hollow, empty caves, repeating each

other almost to infinity, each one the echo and pattern of the one before: an eight-foot-long tunnel leads to a circular room about twenty feet in diameter; inside it is dark but a lighted match reveals that the inner walls of the caves are highly polished and reflect beautiful natural shades and shapes in pink and grey stone. The tunnel is man-made and its walls have been left rough.

The negative emphasis of the novel is here reinforced: there is nothing to see within the caves; they add nothing to the sum of good and evil; the possibility of relationship is negated as the match flame yearns towards its own reflection, touches it and expires; so in the final chapter Aziz and Fielding yearn towards each other, touch, half-kiss and part. The vocabulary echoes that of the first chapter with its 'Ganges. . .sun. . .extraordinary. . .Marabar Caves. . .fists and fingers'.

Chapter 13

Summary

Aziz hopes that Mrs Moore and Adela have forgotten the proposed visit to the caves but when he learns that they have been expecting to hear from him, he issues invitations. The main party is to comprise those who went to tea with Fielding at Government College: Aziz himself, the Principal, Mrs Moore, Adela and Godbole. The problems of such an expedition seem immense to Aziz; first, he is troubled about the picnic: Godbole is a Hindu and will not eat meat, nor can he sit near anyone who may be eating beef; Aziz, as a Mohammedan, will not eat ham or allow others to eat it in his presence; the Europeans may wish for alcohol ('whisky-sodas and ports'!) whilst the Indians will not.

At last, however, all is arranged. Aziz spends the night before the excursion at the station, to make sure he is not late. The first guests to arrive are the two ladies with their servant, Antony, who is promptly sent back, despite his protests that he had been told by Ronny to stay close to his mistresses. There are far too many servants around and some more are sent away by Mohammed Latif, the 'poor relation' who is acting as major-domo.

Whilst they all wait for Fielding and Godbole the train starts very suddenly and Aziz and Mohammed Latif have to leap on the foot-board. As the train steams out of the station the two missing guests are seen, held up at the level-crossing. Fielding tries to jump on the train but misses and falls back on to the line. He is unhurt; nevertheless, Aziz is distraught for he feels that he will be blamed for everything going wrong. Mrs Moore tells him to stop worrying as they are all going to enjoy themselves even without Fielding and Godbole. As the train travels on towards the hills Aziz asks

Mohammed Latif what is in the caves; the old man does not know, though he assures Aziz that the local villagers will act as guides.

Commentary

Yet another attempt to establish relationships between East and West gets underway in this chapter, yet the problems of connection on even the simplest level are underlined by Aziz's worry about food; India is itself divided and communications between Mohammedan and Hindu are often difficult. The belief on the part of the British that Indians are unpunctual and incapable of responsibility is strengthened by Aziz's efforts to prove it wrong; he stays up all night in order to be on time and Godbole misses the train; likewise, the complications of the arrangements and the vast number of servants show the shortcomings, rather than the skill of the organisation.

Religion is again to the forefront and it is shown not to unite but to divide; the food problems arise from religious observances and Godbole misses the train because he 'miscalculated the length of a prayer'. Notice, too, the reference to kites; they are a threat to the stationmaster's hens and may well warn us of worse things to come.

Chapter 14

Summary

The train journey to the Marabar Hills, uneventful in itself, is enlivened by Aziz's attempts to keep his guests happy by such offerings as food and tea, served on a tray by Mahmoud Ali's butler. Adela and Mrs Moore talk about the approach of the hot weather; we learn that Adela and Ronny are to be married in May, by which time it will be so hot that Mrs Moore will have to remain up in the Himalayas until the weather cools, before she will be able to return home to England. Mrs Moore is feeling tired and rather dispirited; she drops asleep as they talk; when she wakes up Adela is looking out of the window and the hills are close by. The sun is about to rise; it promises to be beautiful but just at the moment when day should break it appears to get darker again: it is the false dawn; the actual sunrise is dull and disappointing.

Aziz greets his guests with a warning to put on their topis or sunhats as the morning sun is dangerous. The train goes on past the hills for about a mile into the plain, where it stops at a wayside platform. There, an elephant is waiting. Aziz and his guests and Mohammed Latif mount the elephant and sit in the howdah; with a procession of servants and local villagers they make their way to the caves. An oppressive silence surrounds them, in which there are no echoes; Adela sees what she thinks is a snake; it turns out to be a stump of wood but the villagers insist that it really is a snake.

The plain is left behind and at last they are among the hills; they settle in the shade of a hill where a cloth is laid before them; once again, Mahmoud Ali's butler produces eggs and tea and they are promised breakfast later.

For a while they sit and talk; Aziz is in his element, speaking about the Mogul emperors. Then it is time to fulfil the purpose of their expedition so they go to visit the first cave and everyone crowds into it. Mrs Moore feels faint; a sort of pad seems to settle on her mouth; trying to escape from the cave she strikes her head and finally fights her way to the entrance. However, it is not the noise, smell and crush alone that distress her; in contrast to the silence of the journey, she is aware of a terrifying echo inside the cave which reduces every sound to the same monotonous noise, 'Boum'.

When they are all outside Adela tells her that Aziz wants to go to another cave. Mrs Moore decides to stay behind and rest as she feels unable to face the walk. She suggests that fewer people should be allowed into the next cave so Aziz decides to take only one guide with them. Once they have gone, Mrs Moore begins a letter to her younger children, Ralph and Stella, back in England but she feels weary and depressed; the echo of the cave troubles her and she is unable to rouse herself to any interest in life or in what is around her; somehow her belief in Christianity is nullified so that she ceases to care about anyone or anything.

Commentary

Adela has now accepted her role as a future Anglo-Indian but she is not entirely happy in it; we see her questioning the image of the Anglo-Indian wife who deserts her husband in the hot weather. Mrs Moore, however, is more realistic, pointing out that children cannot be kept on the hot plains throughout the year. During this expedition Mrs Moore is more querulous and more cynical than she has appeared before. She is unwell and rather depressed; Forster is here clearly preparing for her death a short while later. The heat and the crowd and, above all, the echo in the cave have affected her psychologically and she appears to have a mystic experience – or perhaps what we should today see as a nervous breakdown – which makes her lose her faith in Christianity and thus her hold on life.

Throughout his novels Forster manifests a kind of love/hate relationship with modern (that is, of the early decades of the century!) machinery; the car ride in Chapter 8 ends with an accident; here the train journey begins in confusion with half the guests not present and ends slowing up against an elephant. Despite Aziz's pleasure and hospitality, this chapter begins to take on a slightly ominous tone: the imagery of kites and snakes is extended; the sun appears to be hostile; the sky is shown to dominate, 'as usual'; the emptiness and nothingness is emphasised; and, finally, the echo plays a major part in Mrs Moore's breakdown.

Chapter 15

Summary
Aziz, Adela and the guide continue with the expedition but the heat is oppressive so they decide not to climb to the summit. Aziz's thoughts are on the 'English breakfast' being prepared for them, Adela's on Ronny and her marriage to him; she suddenly realises that she does not love him; taken aback, she wonders whether love is, anyway, really necessary to marriage and thinks it is probably not. These thoughts prompt her to ask Aziz if he is married and whether he has children. Then, without realising it, Adela commits a grave social error for Mrs Turton had told her that Mohammedans always have four wives; she asks Aziz if he has more than one wife. Aziz is desperately offended, answers that he has only one and dives into a cave to recover his balance. Absent-mindedly, and not understanding her mistake, Adela also enters a cave.

Commentary
The build-up towards catastrophe now accelerates. In the previous chapter Mrs Moore found that her Christian belief had dissipated itself in the echo of the cave; now Adela understands that she is about to marry without love and Aziz has been affronted.

Notice the ambiguity of the events here: both Adela and Aziz have been forced to think in their different ways about love and marriage and about each other; however, Aziz has already, earlier in the novel, expressed his feelings about Adela's lack of sexual attraction; now it is apparent that Adela is in no way attracted to him. Only after these facts have been established does Forster allow each of them to go into 'a cave'; though he does not specify that it is a different cave, he does not imply that it is the same one.

Chapter 16

Summary
Aziz emerges from his cave smoking; he sees the guide outside listening to the sound of a car on the Chandrapore road. They find a vantage point to look down on it; then Aziz goes to tell Adela what they have seen but he cannot find her. He and the guide search and shout without success: all the caves look the same and Adela has disappeared. Aziz is very distressed and, blaming the guide for neglecting his guest, he strikes him in the face; the man runs away. It is then that Aziz sees Adela at the bottom of the gully talking to people from the car; naïvely, he assumes that she has gone down 'in the hope of a little drive'. He sets off to return to his camp when he catches sight of Adela's field glasses, strap broken, lying in the entrance tunnel of one of the caves; he picks them up and goes on his way.

Back at the camp, Fielding has arrived in the car with Miss Derek, and has gone ahead to find Aziz's party, leaving her with the car and the chauffeur. When Aziz learns this, he prepares to send an escort for Miss Derek. Meanwhile, Mrs Moore asks about Adela and Aziz, trying to avoid the embarrassment of explaining how she had gone away, begins to lie about what happened. At this point Miss Derek's chauffeur comes on the scene to report that she and Adela have returned to Chandrapore. Fielding is angry and blames Adela; Mrs Moore is irritated and blames Miss Derek; Aziz puts a brave face on it and insists that his guests must please themselves, but he is disappointed. He proceeds to elaborate on his cover-up story so that he hardly knows the truth any longer.

They strike camp and leave. On the road Fielding is disturbed because he can see no path from the caves to the place where the car was parked; Aziz claims that there are 'millions'. Fielding is also worried about the expense of the picnic but Aziz makes light of it. When the train arrives back in Chandrapore Mr Haq, the Inspector of Police, is waiting for it; he tries to arrest Aziz, who immediately attempts to escape. Fielding manages to persuade him to go arm in arm with him to McBryde; once outside the station, however, Mr Turton calls Fielding away and Aziz is taken to prison.

Commentary

The arrest of Aziz, which may appear to confirm all the worst criticisms of British behaviour in India, is in fact exactly what would happen in Britain if an accusation such as that which is made in the next chapter were to be made against a man. Forster gains dramatic effect by placing the arrest before our knowledge of the alleged crime.

Throughout this chapter Aziz has gradually invented a story full of circumstantial details which are likely later to rebound upon him. Furthermore, he attempts to resist arrest. His behaviour is typical of the rather emotional Indian character that Forster has portrayed; nevertheless, it is exactly that of someone who is guilty. Fielding's comment, 'Never, never act the criminal', is both a very sensible and a very British way of looking at the situation.

Chapter 17

Summary

Mr Turton calls Fielding into the station waiting-room where, consumed with anger, he tells him that Aziz has assaulted Adela in one of the Marabar Caves. Fielding is at first almost speechless. Then he asks who has made the charge and suggests that Adela is mad; this makes Turton even angrier and he demands that Fielding withdraw the remark. Fielding does so but insists that Aziz is innocent and that the whole matter can be easily cleared up. Turton is beside himself, both at the alleged assault and at Fielding's assumption that Aziz could not possibly be guilty of such an act. He tells Fielding that the matter will be discussed at the Club that evening, whereat Fielding declares that he will be there. The two part. Before returning home Turton steps out on to the platform and puts an end to the looting of Aziz's possessions; for a moment the British side of him – moderate and concerned for justice – prevails. By the time he arrives home he is in a passion again.

Commentary

All the frustrations, irritations and hatreds of the Anglo-Indians now come to the surface. Aziz is guilty in their eyes before he has come to trial. Emotive phrases such as 'a lady, a young lady' and 'an English girl fresh from England' are trotted out to arouse patriotic fervour. Only Fielding sees how preposterous the charge is and attempts to probe its origin.

Chapter 18

Summary

Mr McBryde, the District Superintendent of Police, receives Aziz courteously after his arrest and explains that he must be detained until bail is arranged. Yet he does not for a moment doubt that Aziz is guilty. After leaving Turton, Fielding goes to McBryde, hoping to get some information. McBryde tells him that Adela accuses Aziz of making insulting advances towards her in the cave; she declares that she hit at him with her field-glasses and that, in pulling them away from her, he broke the strap. Of course, they were found in Aziz's pocket and appear to be evidence of the truth of her story. McBryde goes on to say that Adela appears to have been frightened by an echo. He explains that after Fielding had left Miss Derek she saw Adela crashing down the hillside and had gone to help her; he praises Miss Derek's sensible behaviour in bringing Adela straight back to Chandrapore.

McBryde is surprised to learn that Fielding believes Aziz to be innocent. He will not allow him to visit Aziz, though Mahmoud Ali is allowed in. He also prevents Fielding from going to speak to Adela. Whilst they are talking, the table-drawer from Aziz's bungalow, with the photograph of his wife on the top, is brought in as evidence. Though Fielding declares it to be Aziz's wife, McBryde does not believe him.

Commentary

Adela's story appears to suggest Aziz's guilt and, if we are to accept the novelist's earlier account of events, we are left puzzled as to what happened to Adela in the cave. This has led some critics to agree with Fielding's theory that the guide assaulted her; Forster, however, has already shown how Mrs Moore acted completely irrationally in the cave and was both mentally and emotionally affected. He has, therefore, prepared us to accept a similar psychological breakdown in Adela. It would at least be possible to assume (if we have to have an explanation!) that the strap of Adela's field glasses had caught on the rough wall of the entrance tunnel and that this had made her believe she was being attacked; tugging at them in a panic could well have broken the strap.

We should take note of McBryde's complimentary reference to Miss Derek, for later on (Chapter 31) we learn that the two have been having an affair. It is one of the minor ironies of the novel that McBryde, whilst himself committing adultery, is ready, unjustly, to condemn Aziz.

Chapter 19

Summary

When Fielding leaves McBryde's office Hamidullah is waiting outside. He is worried but seems unwilling to make a personal stand on Aziz's behalf. He is, however, determined to involve every influential Indian he can think of; he wants the Nawab Bahadur to stand bail and he particularly chooses Amritrao, a Hindu barrister from Calcutta, to defend the case because of his anti-British attitude. Fielding is unable to persuade Hamidullah to approach the whole matter coolly. They part, swearing friendship, and Fielding sends a message to Aziz, begging him to keep calm.

Fielding returns to Government College where Professor Godbole comes to talk to him, ostensibly about a Russell's viper (a poisonous snake) which had been found in one of the classrooms. At the end of this conversation Godbole asks if the expedition to the caves was a success. Fielding is astonished to find that Godbole can ask such a question, even though he knows about Aziz's arrest. The Professor goes on to remind Fielding that he is about to leave Chandrapore and return to his birthplace in Central India, where he intends to start a high school; he begs Fielding to try to think of a name for his school. Fielding, however, can think of nothing except the recent trouble and he suddenly asks Godbole if Aziz is innocent or guilty. A strange conversation ensues in which Godbole puts forward the philosophy of collective responsibility for good and evil in the world and parries every attempt by Fielding to elicit a straightforward answer.

That afternoon Fielding obtains a permit to see Aziz but Aziz is distressed because Fielding had deserted him at the time of his arrest. Fielding goes home and writes to Adela Quested.

Commentary

A link is being prepared here with Part III which takes us to Mau, Professor

Godbole's birthplace. At the same time the discussion emphasises for us the mystery of India; in Chapter 7 we had seen how Aziz was quite unable to penetrate the mind of Godbole; now it is Fielding's turn to be bewildered.

Chapter 20

Summary
The English women now regret that they had not tried earlier to make Adela welcome. That evening more people than usual go to the Club and there is general discussion and gossip about the situation. Then the women are sent out of the smoking-room; the men, including the subaltern who had played polo with Aziz, remain; they continue the discussion until the door opens and Mr Callendar enters to the accompaniment of Mrs Turton's cry, 'She's better'. From the conversation which follows it appears that Adela was never as sick as the Civil Surgeon had led people to believe. Callendar soon begins to bait Fielding who at first refuses to rise to the challenge. After a few minutes Ronny Heaslop appears and all the men except Fielding stand in deference; this leads to a verbal attack on Fielding who now makes a clear statement of his belief in Aziz's innocence; he immediately resigns from the Club and, after a minor fracas, leaves the room.

Commentary
Since the echo in the caves the use of the structural echo motif has been less prominent but in this chapter echoes arise again. The 'stray subaltern' from Chapter 6 reappears, with his memory of playing polo with an Indian who, though he does not realise, it, was Aziz. Likewise, the parrot-cry of 'women and children' is repeated. However, until the last paragraph the language is fairly business-like, forwarding the story; the final paragraph recalls the Marabar Hills and reminds us of the significance of the sky; with the words 'the cool benediction of the night descended', it reminds us that the Indians seek out the cool and that the hot weather is hostile to life, thus underlining divisions rather than suggesting connections.

Chapter 21

Summary
When Fielding leaves the Club he goes to join his Indian friends, the Nawab Bahadur, Hamidullah and Mahmoud Ali. As he rides to meet them he reflects that he will miss his games of tennis and billiards at the Club and, of the people, probably McBryde, but little else; on the other hand, he will avoid the danger of carrying gossip from the Club to the other side. All around him the excitement of the Mohammedan Feast of Mohurram,

with preparations for the procession through the town, is building up. From the Indians he learns that Amritrao has agreed to be retained for Aziz and that bail is being applied for once again. The discussion is marred by the noise from a group of musicians but when Fielding wants to dismiss them the Nawab Bahadur refuses, believing they might bring good luck.

Fielding returns home and thinks of telling Godbole of his moral error in insulting Ronny but the old Professor has gone to bed. A day or so later he slips off to his new job without seeing Fielding again.

Commentary
This very short chapter marks out clearly for the reader the opposing line-up for the trial: the Englishmen and women at the Club on the one hand, the Mohammedans and Fielding on the other. Godbole, as representative Hindu, withdraws himself from the fray.

Chapter 22

Summary
For days Adela lies in the McBryde's bungalow, sick from a touch of the sun and sore from the cactus spines which had caught in her flesh during her headlong downhill flight from the caves. She goes over and over in her mind the events of that day, remembering particularly how she scratched the wall of the cave with her fingernail to start the echo; it was apparently after this that the alleged assault took place but her whole story is very lacking in firm detail; the most certain aspect of it appears to be the echo. Meanwhile, though she longs to see Mrs Moore, she receives no visit from her.

At last Ronny comes to fetch her away and she is told that she will have to appear in court at the trial and submit to cross-examination by an Indian lawyer. Since it is clear that Ronny cannot hear the case, it will come before his assistant, Das. She now learns what has been going on whilst she has been sick and hears for the first time that Fielding has gone over to the Indian side. McBryde explains that because of this he had opened a letter which Fielding had sent to her, trying to convince her of Aziz's innocence.

When they reach Ronny's bungalow Mrs Moore is not very welcoming and is peculiarly irritated about the demands the young people make on her; she insists that she will not go into the witness-box and she exudes a complete disillusion with life which seems to amount to spiritual despair. Whilst she speaks, Adela, who had been crying, stops suddenly and begins to mutter Aziz's name; then she declares that he is innocent. Ronny, momentarily shocked, looks around to see if any Indian is within earshot. However, Adela's echo has gone and she suggests that the trial should be cancelled and Aziz set free, saying that she heard Mrs Moore affirm Aziz's innocence. Ronny tries to convince her that she has confused Mrs Moore's words with Fielding's letter in which he had stated, 'Aziz is innocent'. They appeal to Mrs Moore who replies that she had never said his name but of course he is innocent. When Ronny begins to cross-question her she again gets very irritated; she insists that Aziz is good and that he did not assault Adela. The seeds of doubt have now crept into Adela's mind but Ronny persuades her that the trial must go on. Mrs Moore's cynical comment about this prompts her son to plan on sending her home immediately.

Commentary
Since the expedition to the caves the reader has heard nothing of Mrs Moore until this chapter. Her experience in the cave appears to have changed her personality for she seems to have lost faith in God and to have become impatient to the point of bitterness with her son and his fiancée. Even so, there is a mystic transmission of thoughts between her and Adela; it cures Adela of her echo, if only briefly, and is eventually to convince her of Aziz's innocence.

Chapter 23

Summary
The ladies of Chandrapore had earlier (Chapter 22) sent a telegram to Lady Mellanby, wife of the Lieutenant-Governor, asking her to intervene to prevent a white woman's case coming before an Indian magistrate. Lady Mellanby is about to sail for England and explains that she is unable to help in this matter; however, she asks if there is anything else she can do to assist. The upshot of this is that she offers accommodation in her own cabin to enable Mrs Moore to return home immediately. Thus, Mrs Moore leaves Chandrapore before the trial and before her son's marriage and she escapes the hot weather. Since Ronny is unable to leave Chandrapore, she travels westwards across central India to Bombay alone. There she embarks on the homeward journey with Lady Mellanby.

Commentary
This chapter is more concerned with Mrs Moore's inner thoughts than with her physical removal from India. It suggests that she is physically frail and spiritually sick. She has not recovered from the nihilism of her experience in the Marabar Caves and her musings about love are expressions of regret for what she feels she no longer possesses. Before the Marabar expedition her references to Christianity and the Bible had been those of hope; the shift to the Book of Lamentations (1.12) in her reference to sorrow marks

the change to despair. It may also prepare us for the role of god which the Indians impose on Mrs Moore; the sorrow of Lamentations is God's sorrow.

Chapter 24

Summary
The day of the trial arrives and the heat with it. Adela, who has been staying with the Turtons since Mrs Moore's departure, is far from happy; her echo has returned and she is convinced that she will break down in court. Mr Turton, however, assures her that she will win and they all set out for the courthouse together. There they congregate in Ronny's private room, together with the other English people involved in the trial. When the case is called, special chairs are taken into the court for them and they file in. Adela notices first the punkah-wallah, physically a magnificent figure but an 'untouchable', a member of the lowest and most degraded class in India; throughout the trial he pulls the rope which works the punkah, or fan, aware of nothing but the rhythmic action he performs.

McBryde opens the case for the prosecution; with a bored air, he goes over the events of the Marabar expedition. When an unkind remark from an unknown member of the crowd makes Adela tremble, Major Callendar promptly asks for her to be accommodated on the platform on medical grounds. The magistrate, Das, allows this but immediately all the English present, except for Fielding, also climb on to the platform. This leads to an argument with Mahmoud Ali, defending Aziz, and Das asks the English to leave the platform which, after some bitter altercation, they do. The case continues until McBryde suggests that Mrs Moore was deliberately ill-treated in the first cave in order to ensure that Aziz and Adela would not have her company in the next. Another argument develops over the fact that Mrs Moore has gone home and is unable to speak on either side. During this disagreement Mahmoud Ali passes his papers over to Amritrao and leaves the court dramatically. Meanwhile, outside, the incantation 'Esmiss Esmoor' is heard, deifying Mrs Moore.

The cross-examination of Adela begins; as each question is asked she re-enacts the details of the Marabar trip in her mind, replying as she sees each event occur. When she is asked whether Aziz followed her into the cave she waits to see him do so in her mind's eye but he does not appear; she now realises that this is the truth - he did not follow her! She announces that she has made a mistake and pandemonium breaks loose. Mr Callendar tries to stop the trial on medical grounds but Das knows that he has now to force the prosecution to withdraw the charge. At last McBryde says that he withdraws and Das releases Aziz 'without one stain on his character'. Everyone rushes out of the courtroom except the punkah-wallah who continues to pull on his rope, unaware that anything unusual has happened.

Commentary

The account of the trial is a caricature but Forster wishes to illustrate the spirit of Anglo-Indian attitudes, not necessarily actual events. He avoids presenting a complete travesty of justice since the outcome of the trial, thanks to Adela's inner core of honesty, completely vindicates Aziz. Simultaneously, it shows us that, despite their passionate feelings, the Anglo-Indians accept the decision of the court.

The deification of Mrs Moore which occurs here is part of the mystic thread which runs through the novel. Though neither the reader nor the protagonists know it at this point, when the chant of 'Esmiss Esmoor' is taken up, Mrs Moore is already dead; yet her spirit informs much of the action which is to follow.

Chapter 25

Summary

The court breaks up in disorder and the victorious Indians rampage through the streets of Chandrapore. Adela gets separated from the other English; when she chances to get thrown against Fielding, he realises that she may be in danger and places her in his own carriage. His servant, however, has taken the horses and gone to visit a friend, so Fielding feels compelled to stay with Adela. Then a group of his students arrive and insist on acting as his horses; they pull the carriage in the procession which is escorting Aziz but suddenly they turn aside towards Government College and there they leave it. Fielding takes Adela inside only to find that the telephone wires have been cut and he cannot get into touch with McBryde. He provides her with a couple of rooms and with drinks and biscuits and, feeling very frustrated, he lies down to rest.

Meanwhile, Aziz has missed him and is unhappy because his one English friend is absent from the celebrations. Mahmoud Ali is in an ugly mood and anxious to attack the English. Using the Nawab Bahadur's nephew, Nureddin, as an excuse, he proposes an attack on Mr Callendar at the hospital, asserting that Nureddin has been tortured. At the hospital Dr Panna Lal manages to avert disaster by acting the clown. Nureddin is brought out and they all proceed to the Nawab Bahadur's town house, with the intention of going on to his country house in the evening when it is cooler. The Nawab himself announces that he intends to give up his title and become plain Mr Zulfiqar.

Commentary

Despite the considerable confusion and the Indians' threats, little harm seems to be done. Even Adela is fêted when she is seen riding in the carriage with Fielding. Yet this is the true sign of the division between English and

Indians for Fielding knows that were Adela to be attacked he would have
to defend her, though he feels nothing for her; he would defend her against
Aziz and his Indian friends, though they mean more to him than she does.

Chapter 26

Summary
Fielding awakes in the evening to find that Adela is still at Government
College. Though he makes it quite clear that he is not interested, she tries
to explain herself to him; in so doing she claims that she has been unwell
for some time but that in court the echo – the buzzing sound in her ears –
disappeared. They agree that there are four possibilities to explain the
event at the caves: that Aziz is guilty; that Adela invented the charge out
of malice; that she had an hallucination; that someone else, perhaps the
guide, committed the offence. The first two explanations they discount.
Whilst they discuss the last two, Hamidullah arrives. He is resentful towards
Adela and objects to her remaining at Government College when Fielding
joins his Indian friends at Dilkusha, the Nawab Bahadur's country place.

Now Ronny arrives with news that Mrs Moore died soon after her ship
left Bombay. Adela is very distressed at this and decides that she does not
want to be with Ronny. She is finally left at Government College while
Hamidullah and Fielding go off to a victory dinner at Dilkusha, having first
agreed not to spoil Aziz's evening by telling him of Mrs Moore's death. On
the way there Fielding learns with horror that Amritrao is considering
claiming twenty thousand rupees in compensation for Aziz from Adela.

Commentary
By now the echo in the caves has been clearly equated with evil and it is
significant that when Adela faces the truth during the trial her echo disappears. Even before the announcement of Mrs Moore's death, this chapter
has been concerned with the problems of death and heaven and the question of the validity of the supernatural; the idea of ghosts recurs and is
immediately associated with Mrs Moore whose ghostly (that is, spiritual)
presence is to remain a dominating factor throughout the rest of the book.

Chapter 27

Summary
After the victory dinner, Fielding and his Indian friends lie on the roof
beneath their mosquito nets and prepare to sleep. Aziz and Fielding begin
to talk and Fielding tries to persuade Aziz not to claim exorbitant damages
from Adela. Fielding has for one evening become an Indian, has dressed
himself in native costume and eaten their food; yet he is aware that, deep

32

within himself he, the Westerner, can never truly acquire the essence of the Indian spirit. He tries to explain to Aziz the courage that it must have taken for Adela to recant but Aziz refuses to understand. The disagreement between the two changes course when Aziz announces that he will consult Mrs Moore about damages. He goes on to say that he keeps forgetting she has left India and that when her name was chanted during the trial he fancied she was present. Fielding is puzzled at Aziz's devotion to Mrs Moore and troubled because he knows that she is dead. Suddenly he blurts this out to Aziz but Hamidullah, who has been listening to their conversation, says it is a joke. Aziz, used to such jokes, refuses to believe that Mrs Moore is truly dead. Fielding says no more; he remains quiet, contemplating the problem of death: he thinks that, whilst people are believed to be alive, they possess some sort of immortality; he feels, too, that he has just tried to kill Mrs Moore there on the roof, give her 'the final blow', but he is conscious that she still eludes him.

Commentary
The perplexing and mystic aspect of the novel is gaining power. The question of compensation is unimportant when compared with the philosophical problems of life and death. Mrs Moore has again taken over: we left Adela thinking of her at Government College; now she is in the minds of Fielding, Aziz and Hamidullah; alive or dead, her influence reaches out to affect the lives of all the rest; when Aziz felt her presence at the trial she was already dead, yet the reader is aware that she was, in some indefinable way, there with both Aziz and Adela.

Chapter 28

Summary and commentary
This short chapter is concerned with the effect of Mrs Moore's death. Lady Mellanby, who had kindly offered her accommodation in her cabin is shocked and distressed but she hardly knew her and when the ship at last begins to move northwards the death on board is gradually forgotten.

In Chandrapore, however, a legend arises around the death; Mrs Moore is deified and her tomb is identified in various places around the city. Ronny Heaslop feels guilty about his mother's death but he pushes his conscience aside, remembering that she was very troublesome to him in India: she had been a bad influence on Adela and had actually allowed herself to get mixed up with the Indians. The reference to Ronny's religion confirms the earlier comments made in Chapter 5 and should recall to us that there Mrs Moore had been reminded of his public school days; the complacency, the lack of regret she had seen in him then, may be compared with his attitude now. He is ready to dismiss the memory of his

mother with a memorial tablet in her church at home; at the same time he
is anxious to dismiss Adela with as little ceremony; he determines to 'ask
her to release him' as soon as the claim for damages is settled.

Chapter 29

Summary

The troubles which follow the trial are such that Sir Gilbert Mellanby, the
Lieutenant-Governor of the Province, visits the area. He praises Fielding,
condemns some of the others and leaves them to settle the question of
damages.

Fielding lodges with Hamidullah and Adela remains at the College; the
other Anglo-Indians refuse to have anything to do with her. With Fielding's
help she writes a personal apology to Aziz but he still sticks to his intention of claiming a large sum in compensation. Then Fielding tries to use
Aziz's affection for Mrs Moore to change his mind. Suddenly Aziz gives in,
convinced that Mrs Moore would want him to spare her son's fiancée; he
goes from one extreme to the other, refusing now to claim anything but
his costs. Despite his generous gesture, the English people give him no
credit for it and they continue to believe that he is guilty.

After everything has been settled Ronny breaks off the engagement and
it is arranged that Adela will return home. In a final conversation, Fielding
and Adela find they like each other; they agree to write and perhaps even
meet should Fielding ever take home leave. Then Adela follows the route
Mrs Moore took homewards. On the way there she decides that her first
duty once back in England is to look up Mrs Moore's other two children,
Ralph and Stella.

Commentary

The plot now begins to fizzle out: Mrs Moore is dead, Adela back in
England and the trial is over; yet the echoes of love and life and death
continue to reverberate; the reader is left uneasy, feeling that much has
happened but little has been settled.

Chapter 30

Summary

A favourable consequence of the trial is that the Hindus and Moslems try
to get on with each other better. One day the magistrate, Das, visits Aziz
at the hospital and asks two favours: a remedy for shingles and a poem for
Mr Bhattacharya's new magazine, intended not for Hindus but for Indians
generally. Aziz gives him a prescription and promises a poem but it never
gets written. However, his discussion with Das and his disillusionment

following his imprisonment and trial determine him to leave British India and seek a post in a Hindu state. Hamidullah tries to persuade him that this would be a foolish move since he would earn less money and never become rich enough to educate his children and advance his own medical career. However, Aziz explains that it is not in his character to acquire wealth and he would sooner take a poor job and have the chance to write poetry.

The conversation turns to Adela as Hamidullah points out that Aziz could have had money had he made Adela pay. Hamidullah then tells him the local gossip that Fielding had visited Adela late at night when she was staying at the College. Aziz brushes the story aside but his sudden explosion of nerves which follows shows that he is more moved than he likes to confess. Hamidullah then persuades him that they should both go behind the purdah to see his wife and Nureddin's mother who is on a visit.

Commentary

The attempt to heal the breach between Moslem and Hindu only serves to emphasise the divisions between them. Das and Aziz, both cultured and educated, are outwardly friendly towards each other but they cannot control their inner prejudices; notice how Aziz again associates cow-dung with the Hindus. Furthermore, the discussion about purdah shows that, even if the more intelligent men wish to put an end to it, the women need to be educated and enlightened before they are willing to abandon it.

Chapter 31

Summary

Whilst Fielding is away at a conference Aziz broods upon the rumour about him and Adela; after a while he assumes it to be true. An avowed scandal has arisen in the British community: Mr McBryde has been caught in Miss Derek's room and his wife is divorcing him. When Fielding returns, Aziz tells him of this scandal; he then adds that there is gossip about him and Adela. Fielding does not even bother to deny the story because he does not expect Aziz to believe it. As soon as it becomes clear that Aziz accepts the story, Fielding refutes it and angrily calls his Indian friend a little rotter, which cuts Aziz to the quick. Such misunderstandings arise too easily and, though Aziz appears to be appeased, he makes excuses to get out of a dinner arrangement he has made with Fielding; the excuses are not accepted and Fielding insists that they stand by their arrangement.

Mr Turton meets Fielding at the Post Office and tells him that he is expected at the Club that evening as the Lieutenant-Governor has insisted on his reinstatement. Fielding attends reluctantly; there he meets Callendar's and Ronny Heaslop's replacements and reflects that changes have been made in name only; otherwise it is all the same. He leaves to fulfil his engagement with Aziz; over dinner they talk about poetry and religion and about Fielding's plan to go on leave. Aziz asks him if he will see Adela Quested; when Fielding replies that he will if he has time, Aziz feels depressed and sick and returns home. He convinces himself that Fielding is going to England to marry Adela and he decides to avoid seeing his English friend again. Next day he takes his children back to Mussoorie. Fielding writes Aziz a letter, trying to explain himself but he receives only a cold reply. He leaves for England, and Aziz, back in Chandrapore again, persuades himself that Fielding is already married to Adela.

Commentary
All hopes of connection seem to have dissolved. The blossoming friendship between Aziz and Fielding is destroyed through suspicion and misunderstanding. The evil of the echo is prominent; the new administration echoes the old, offering no hope for love and reconciliation.

Chapter 32

Summary and commentary
On his journey homeward Fielding stops for a few days in Egypt and is refreshed by its simplicity and clarity. He goes on, visiting Crete and Italy, and he feels a sense of disloyalty to India in the pleasure he takes in the beauty of form he finds in Europe, particularly in the Italian churches. As he writes postcards to his Indian friends he realises that they would neither understand nor appreciate the beauty and harmony he finds in Venice. The difference between them is underlined by this fact and we are aware as Part II draws to a close that it is the author, as much as Fielding, who is rejoicing in the glories of classical Europe.

2.3 PART III – TEMPLE

Chapter 33

Summary and commentary
Two years have passed; the scene has now changed to a Hindu State some hundred miles to the west of Chandrapore and the Marabar Hills. The protagonists have not changed, however. Professor Godbole, now Minister of Education, is helping to celebrate the Festival of the Birth of Krishna at the palace of Mau. Forster's description of the ceremony is designed to show the rich confusion of the occasion. The first paragraph illustrates the philosophic muddle of a Birth myth and comparisons with the origins of Christianity are made obvious as the account proceeds by such

comments as 'Gokul (the Bethlehem in that nebulous story)', 'King Kansa, who is Herod' and 'the father and mother of the Lord, warned to depart in a dream'.

Godbole celebrates the birth by singing and dancing and by 'imitating God' in bringing into his own spiritual ambience 'all men, the whole universe'. Whilst he is doing this, Mrs Moore comes into his mind, closely followed by a wasp he had once seen and we remember how in Chapter 3 Mrs Moore had extended her simple Christian love to the wasp on her peg. When the aged and sick ruler of the State is brought in the festival reaches its climax in the birth and naming of the baby god; the inevitable snake, in the shape of a papier-mâché cobra, is present. Only after this, when the Rajah is taken back to his own quarters, are we reintroduced to Dr Aziz, now the official court physician, who administers a sedative to the sick old man.

The people continue to rejoice, playing games and indulging in jokes, for Forster points out that Hindu worship includes merriment, which is missing from Christianity. The chapter ends with Professor Godbole reflecting on the merrymaking, remembering again Mrs Moore and echoing the words of the song he had sung for her at Fielding's tea party in Chapter 7. Only when he leaves the palace do we realise that it is raining outside and that Part III completes the cycle of the Indian seasons, taking place in the rains, the season of life and hope.

Chapter 34

Summary

Aziz leaves the palace at the same time as Godbole; seeing the Professor ahead of him he greets him, only to be at first rebuffed by Godbole waving his arms to indicate that he does not wish to be disturbed. Aziz's apology, however, evokes the response from Godbole that 'he' has arrived at the European Guest House. No further information is offered but Aziz knows that 'he' is Fielding who is coming on an official visit to inspect the education of the province. Aziz is now fully convinced that Fielding is married to Adela; he had, in fact, received a letter which announced Fielding's marriage but he had not read it through; he had simply thrown it across to Mahmoud Ali and asked him to answer it. It had strengthened his hatred of the English and, with the help of Professor Godbole, he had left Chandrapore and taken the post at Mau which he now holds. Though it is a Hindu province he is able to live there quite happily; the climate is pleasant, his children are able to be with him all the year round and he has married again.

Fielding has written to Godbole about his visit; he explains in the letter that he is travelling together with his wife and her brother. Aziz receives the information from Godbole who has also told him that his religious duties at this time will prevent him from arranging anything for Fielding's party.

Commentary
The divisions between Hindu and Moslem referred to in the earlier parts are again set out clearly; at the same time it is suggested that peaceful coexistence between fellow Indians is possible. Aziz lives comfortably among the Hindu community and does not appear to be constantly troubled by the smell of cow-dung, which is not mentioned. For Aziz the major rift is between him and the English but it is quite clear that he has allowed misunderstandings to grow; for instance, he has made no attempt to read Fielding's letters.

Chapter 35

Summary
There exists in Mau the legend of a young Mohammedan whose mother had told him to free prisoners. He had, therefore, gone to the fort and released the prisoners but the police were annoyed and cut off his head. His headless body returned to his mother's door where it fell lifeless. He was declared a saint and consequently two shrines, one of the Head and one of the Body, exist in Mau. The Shrine of the Body is in Aziz's garden. A short walk away, up the hill by the fort, is the Shrine of the Head; it is there that Aziz takes his three children the morning after the Birth of Krishna.

There has been an enormous downpour of rain; the sky still looks black and full of rain-clouds, promising a bumper harvest. At the fort Ahmed and Karim, the two boys, chase around; they see a line of prisoners and ask who is to be pardoned, for that very evening the chief Hindu god will release one prisoner. The prison-guard asks Aziz about the health of the Rajah and is told that it is improving. The truth is, however, that the old ruler is dead but it has been decided to withhold the announcement of his death until the festivities are over.

The boys now see Fielding and his brother-in-law coming up to the Shrine. The Englishmen enter the screening wall and immediately rush out, followed by a swarm of bees. Fortunately, the rain begins again at this moment and the bees disappear. Aziz, who had not intended to speak to them, greets them in some amusement. He pulls a couple of stings out of the wrist of the younger man and promises to send an embrocation over to the Guest House. Fielding asks him why he had not answered his letters but receives no answer because the rain becomes so torrential that they all rush down to the road. As they talk, Aziz constantly verges on the insolent and when they reach Fielding's carriage he exclaims, 'Jump in, Mr Quested, and Mr Fielding'. It is then that his mistake is realised. It transpires that Fielding has married, not Adela but Mrs Moore's daughter, Stella. Aziz is covered in confusion but he refuses to patch up the quarrel, declaring that he wants no English friends. Nevertheless, when he arrives home he is happy and excited at his memories of Mrs Moore and he recollects that he had once promised that he would be kind to Stella and Ralph.

Commentary

The preoccupation with religion continues and the narration moves easily from the Hindu festival to the worship of Mohammed, suggesting again the possibility of religious harmony. Part III of the novel is full of healing and hope and Aziz's hatred of the English seems out of place. Now a chance of reconciliation occurs: Aziz is made aware of his mistake and Mrs Moore's name has recalled to him a relationship he had rejoiced in. Though he has addressed his one-time friend as 'Mr Fielding' he is thinking of him as 'Cyril' again by the end of the chapter.

Chapter 36

Summary

The festival goes on throughout the day and in the evening Aziz remembers that he had promised to send some embrocation against the bee-stings over to the Guest House. He decides to take it himself. On the way he meets Godbole; in a brief conversation he learns that Godbole has known for over a year that Fielding was married to Stella Moore. They separate and, as he proceeds, Aziz observes a boat on the water close to the palace; he guesses that it is the Guest House party. He goes on, however, thinking that he might learn something, if only by questioning the servants.

When he arrives at the Guest House the whole place seems to be deserted. Looking around, he finds two letters – one from Ronny Heaslop and one from Adela – and reads them both without a qualm of conscience. From Ronny's letter we learn that Fielding has a baby son. The notion that all these English people are closing their ranks against the Indians irritates him into thumping the keyboard of the piano and the noise he makes brings an unexpected response. Ralph Moore has been left behind to rest. The boy is mentally retarded, strange-looking and prematurely aged. Aziz is rough with him at first but soon sees that, like his mother Mrs Moore, Ralph has a deep, instinctive understanding of human character. The thought of Mrs Moore changes Aziz's attitude and he offers to take Ralph out in the other boat to see the torchlight procession. He finds himself telling Ralph that the Rajah is dead, a secret he should have told no one; he is very anxious

to show the boy everything at Mau, though he really does not understand
what the religious festival is about. Suddenly their boat collides with that
of Fielding and his wife and they are all four flung into the warm, shallow
water.

Commentary
Here, Aziz finds himself once more under Mrs Moore's spell; though he
intended to have nothing to do with the visiting English party, Ralph's
simplicity and sensitivity move Aziz to use the same words to him that he
had used long ago to Mrs Moore in the mosque, 'Then you are an Oriental'.
This is an acknowledgement of a relationship deeper than mere friendship
for it suggests a oneness that Aziz and Fielding have never achieved. 'Mrs
Moore's son' is a name sacred to Aziz, like that of Mrs Moore herself
(Chapter 37). Notice that cow-dung appears again but now it is part of a
'contented Indian evening'; it is not seen as foul and smelly but is 'burning
eternally'.

Chapter 37

Summary
The accident on the water brings Aziz and Fielding together again. Before
Fielding's party leaves, he and Aziz go for a last ride together in the Mau
jungles. Though the main purpose of his visit was to see the King-Emperor
George Fifth High School, Fielding has been constantly frustrated by
Godbole's excuses; now Aziz confesses that the school has been converted
into a granary. As they ride between bushes and rocks a cobra crawls
across their path. They feel happy together and Aziz produces a letter to
send to Adela, in which he thanks her for her courage at the trial. He
explains to Fielding that he wants to make up for his unkindness and hasty
conclusions by being kind to everyone. Fielding suggests that Aziz should
talk to Stella or even to Ralph because they have a special sort of insight
and understanding; Aziz, however, feels he has nothing to say to them.
    The conversation turns to Hinduism. Neither of the two know much
about it so they move on to politics and wrangle all the way back to Mau.
Though it is essentially a friendly squabble, Aziz gets excited and Fielding
mocks him. Aziz wants nationhood for India; he feels that only when the
English have been driven out, can he and Fielding (or their successors) be
friends. As he says this he rides against Fielding, half-kissing him. Fielding
holds him affectionately, asking why they cannot become friends now.
Time and place, the countryside and nature are against them, however; the
horses swerve apart, rocks separate them and the whole universe appears to
cry out, 'No, not yet' and 'No, not there'.

Commentary

The temporary reconciliation of this last chapter shows what is possible but it is not allowed to be final. Just as the flame from the match in Chapter 12 bends to its own reflection, touches and expires, so here Aziz and Fielding move towards each other, touch and part. The ending, like the opening of the novel is negative, the circular pattern echoing the serpent with its tail in its mouth, but the words 'yet' and 'there' seem to offer hope: though friendship between Aziz and Fielding cannot flourish in this time and place, perhaps in the future harmony can be achieved.

3 THEMES AND ISSUES

3.1 THE PLOT

There is little action in *A Passage to India*. The two banner headlines 'Indian doctor accused of assault on English girl' and 'Case against Indian doctor dismissed' could be said to sum up the whole of its plot. Yet much happens in the realms of the mind and the spirit: friendships form and dissolve; connections are made and broken; the intangible soul of India is approached but remains at the last inviolable. To the readers of Forster's earlier novels the basic outline is familiar: individuals and groups are set in opposition to one another and our interest lies in seeing how things sort themselves out.

The book is made up of three parts – Mosque, Caves, Temple – corresponding, as Forster himself explained, to the three Indian seasons, cold weather, hot weather and rains. There are three major settings, Chandrapore, the Marabar and Mau. The whole of the first short chapter is devoted to describing Chandrapore and the Civil Station, introducing the Marabar Caves and simultaneously showing us the barriers which divide Indians and Anglo-Indians and preparing us to understand the subtle power of the weather and the seasons. The physical features of the landscape are brought vividly before us. The filthy, sprawling, unhygienic Indian city of Chandrapore, with its sordid bazaars and mean houses, lies in the valley along an uninviting stretch of the Ganges; it is looked down upon by both the Eurasians and the English, seeming to fit in with the moral climate which labels the Indians as inferior. The description helps to establish the tone of the novel; the city is dull and ugly, human life of little account; the Civil Station above is neat and prosaic, clean, orderly and 'sensibly planned', sharing 'nothing with the city except the overarching sky'. The surrounding countryside is flat and uninteresting, except where the Marabar Hills seem to add a little excitement to the scenery. Even native India itself is filled with rifts and dissensions, 'a hundred

Indias' which cannot easily be reconciled with each other. It is the disunity within the Anglo-Indian camp, however, which sparks off the trouble.

Despite the differences in wealth, comfort and social standing, subjugators and subjugated in Chandrapore live together in an uneasy peace. The British never question their own superiority and the Indians have learned to live their own lives apart, working with and for their rulers and withdrawing in their leisure time into the company of their own kind. Mrs Moore and Adela Quested, fresh from Britain, with their liberal and Christian ideas unshaped by any realistic awareness of life in Anglo-India, provide a catalyst.

Adela claims that she wants to see 'the *real* India' but what she is seeking is a figment of her own imagination, an Indian version of her own life in suburban England, where visits are exchanged and outings undertaken. She believes that it is possible to establish social contacts which can give her an insight into Indian life, so that 'catching the moon in the Ganges' (Chapter 3) will no longer symbolise her only genuine experience of India. Mrs Moore, on the other hand, more tolerant, with fewer expectations, is more open to accept the impressions which offer themselves. When she goes into the mosque and meets Aziz she accepts him at his own valuation as a human being; retelling her encounter to Ronny, it does not occur to her to indicate 'by the tone of her voice' that the young doctor she had met was an Indian. Nevertheless, both Adela and Mrs Moore are at variance with the prevailing British attitudes, for they have not understood the compulsions and fears which decree that the two nations must remain divided.

Every formal attempt to connect appears to be doomed to failure. The deliberate replication of the accidentally forged link between Mrs Moore and Aziz proves impossible though, it would seem, not for want of trying. Yet, when Mr Turton arranges his Bridge Party it is designed to 'amuse' Adela, not to bring the two nations together in genuine friendship. Even so, from it spring two further opportunities for connections to be made: the first of these, the proposed visit of Mrs Moore and Adela to the Bhattacharyas is a non-starter, a face-saving invitation not meant to be taken seriously; the two English ladies have not been in India long enough to understand the niceties of Indian social behaviour; the invitation itself is a polite gesture and therefore a connection of sorts; the Bhattacharyas do not expect it to be followed up.

The second opportunity is more realistic, for Fielding's carefully planned tea party is designed to bring together English, Anglo-Indian, Moslem and Hindu in an informal atmosphere and on personal terms. Success appears possible: Aziz is articulate, Godbole affable and the English both charmed and responsive; Fielding has no hesitation in leaving Adela to smoke and talk with his two Indian guests whilst he himself takes Mrs Moore on a tour of the College. Such harmony, perfectly acceptable in England, is, however, unconventional on the soil of Anglo-India and the party is rudely broken up by Ronny Heaslop before friendship and understanding can be cemented.

Despite the inimical atmosphere at the end of Fielding's tea party, it has, in its turn, opened the way for Aziz to make overtures. He rashly invites Mrs Moore and Adela to visit him at home but, like the Bhattacharyas, he does not expect them to respond. Though lively and intelligent, his role as Westernised man is confused with his Indian identity – whilst the Europeans expect scrupulously to adhere to arrangements made, the Indians are satisfied with the gesture itself. Thus, the invitation to the Marabar Caves is likewise tossed off with little forethought, a procrastinating measure which Aziz immediately relegates to an obscure corner of his mind. When he feels forced to follow it through the problems which arise make him unhappily aware that he has 'challenged the spirit of the Indian earth, which tries to keep men in compartments' (Chapter 13).

The Bridge Party and Fielding's tea party had taken place in the cold weather when life in India is at its best. Now the approaching hot weather begins to make people nervous; the possibility of an outbreak of cholera fills the inhabitants of Chandrapore with fear and the increasing heat lies over them as a threat. It is an inauspicious moment for Aziz's expedition. The grains of comfort held out in Part I by the various religious creeds – Moslem, Christian and Hindu – are snatched away in the nihilism of the first chapter (Chapter 12) of Part II. Whilst the Mosque appeared to allow the hope of friendship, the Caves are empty, hollow, inimical to Man; they reject individuality; they reject relationship; they add nothing 'to the sum of good or evil'. The attempt to defy their indifference becomes a catastrophe which rocks Chandrapore to its foundations; yet the cause of the trouble seems to be a non-event. In Chapter 1 the caves appeared to excite interest as something extraordinary; they were given a sense of life by the humanising effect of their 'fists and fingers'. Before Aziz's expedition gets under way we are invited to consider the Marabar, and particularly the caves, in greater detail. Again the tone is set by the description: not only are the caves hollow and empty but they also negate all life that enters them. However, the expedition has been planned and must go ahead. The train takes the party across the plains, circles round indeterminately, and drops them an elephant-ride away from the caves; an oppressive, echoless silence accompanies them as they approach their goal, only to be translated in the caves themselves into a meaningless echo which, because it destroys individuality, also destroys hope and renders life hollow and pointless. The reader is thus prepared for the catastrophe which occurs there, a catastrophe which lacks reality but which nullifies the dream of friendship between Indian and English.

What happens to Adela Quested in the cave? If we are to trust the narration (and nothing else occurs to put it in doubt), Aziz is certainly innocent of any assault for we remain with him as he enters a cave, lights a cigarette and, now calmer, goes out to find the guide standing alone, listening to the sound of Miss Derek's car. Adela we do not follow as she too goes into a cave; what experience she has there we can only surmise and, ultimately the actual physical experience is unimportant. Later, after the trial, she and Fielding analyse the situation as they see it. Of the four possibilities they propose they are left with two: either some other person, perhaps the guide, committed the assault, or Adela had an hallucination. Yet at the trial when under cross-examination, Adela watches with her mind's eye for Aziz to follow her into the cave, she sees no one behind her, not Aziz, not the guide, not anyone. If we must have a solution to the mystery, then some sort of hallucination appears to be the only answer.

The atmosphere of the journey, the heat, the strange echoless silence of the Marabar plains culminate for Mrs Moore in her uncanny experience within the first cave. There she feels that she is being attacked; she loses control and fights her way out of the cave, only to be left with the memory of an annihilating echo which gradually destroys her hold on life. Her faith seems to recede from her and she knows that she is going to be ill. This experience has much in common with Adela's: both believe that they are being attacked; both feel ill; both are left with an echo which undermines their normally sane approach to life.

Whatever happens in the cave, however, certainly destroys any fragile connections that have been made. The real catastrophe is spiritual, not physical. Though Aziz is vindicated at the trial, doubt and suspicion cause the budding friendship between him and Fielding to fade; Mrs Moore dies on her voyage homeward; even the engagement between Adela and Ronny Heaslop is broken off. Fielding and Adela return separately to England and Aziz leaves Chandrapore.

Part III of the novel takes place two years later and several hundred miles to the west of the Marabar Hills. From the nihilism and spiritual aridity of the caves it recalls us to a consciousness of the religious life of India. Just as Part I is entitled 'Mosque' after the Moslem place of worship, this part is called 'Temple' for the Hindus. It is set in the princely state of Mau where a number of the protagonists from the earlier parts now gather: Professor Godbole is Minister of Education, Aziz is Court Physician and Fielding is on an official tour to inspect the education of the States of Central India. Here, in this Hindu region, British influence is negligible and the mystery and muddle of India is given free rein. At a time of festival the confusion is accentuated; the elegant palace is crudely decorated with coloured rags and glass balls; the Hindu crowds spill over from the corridor where the festivities are taking place into the palace courtyard and adjoining corridors; everywhere is ablaze with light; the noise of drums and cymbals accompanies Professor Godbole's choir, which finds itself in competition with a Europeanised band playing a waltz. The religious ceremony of the Birth of Krishna is a signal for games and jollity. Though the physical features are unclear, the chaotic events of this part set the scene.

Yet, behind all the outward show, the ancient Rajah is dying, indeed dies before the celebrations are over, emphasising to us the closeness of birth and death; likewise, the thoughts of death and afterlife are brought firmly before us when Godbole impels into his mind the image of Mrs Moore. Nevertheless, the foreboding and disaster of the two previous parts are completely dissipated in the carefree happiness which is part and parcel of the religious rejoicings. The arrival of Fielding and his party, however, recalls us to British fastidiousness: the State Guest House is clearly neglected, its mosquito nets torn, stocks of food inadequate; the oars from the boat are missing; Ralph is stung by bees. The confrontation between Aziz and Fielding brings about a change in the atmosphere which threatens the possibility of reconciliation between the two nations. But it is a time of hope; the rains will result in a bumper harvest; the Birth of Krishna is a festival of love; and the spirit of Mrs Moore hovers around Aziz, recalling the warmth of his affection for her and transferring it to her son Ralph. She is present with Professor Godbole in his religious dance; she lives again through the chants of the Hindu worshippers as they call upon the names of their gods.

As this final chance of reconciliation between East and West is offered, the misunderstandings of the past are sorted out and the tolerance and love of Mrs Moore reassert themselves. The novel ends without positive harmony but in hope; though the time and the place are not propitious for friendship between Aziz and Fielding, one day and somewhere their successors may achieve it.

3.2 POLITICAL ASPECTS

Though Forster himself maintained that his main purpose in *A Passage to India* 'was not political, was not even sociological' (Prefatory Note to 1957 Everyman edition, republished in the Penguin Modern Classics edition, 1979), most of the early reviewers and critics insisted on seeing it as such. Certainly in the mid-1920s it touched a raw spot on the sensibilities of the British Empire builders. Now, however, the India of the novel has gone forever; even the geographical entity that was then India is no longer the same and the political situation has become an historical, though it is no longer a political, fact. Yet the politics of suppression and subjugation are still with us today and they certainly constitute one of Forster's themes.

The Anglo-Indians as a group are little more than caricatures, as is indicated by their introduction to us through the conversation of the Indians in Chapter 2: 'Red-nose mumbles, Turton talks distinctly, Mrs Turton takes bribes, Mrs Red-nose does not and cannot, because so far there is no Mrs Red-nose'. When we actually meet them our impression remains unchanged; with their cosy comedies, their endless drinks and their exaggerated contempt for the Indians they are, for the most part, mere parodies of colonial administrators; Hamidullah's remark that every Englishman becomes the same 'be he Turton or Burton' (Chapter 2) is echoed by Fielding much later in Chapter 30, with his 'Turtons and Burtons are all the same'; and when, after the trial, the individual persons of the administration are replaced, he muses that 'the more the Club changed the more it promised to be the same thing' (Chaper 31).

We are left with the uneasy feeling that Forster has successfully characterised the spirit, if not the fact, of colonial administration, that though individuals may be understanding and compassionate, the generality is not. The worst aspects of colonialism are shown in the unintelligent and biased comments of the Club women and in their lack of courtesy and consideration, even for the superior and educated Indians. Yet the theory of government is exemplary; the Lieutenant-Governor holds enlightened opinions and deplores racial prejudice (Chapter 29); the practice is at fault.

The Indians as a group are likewise typecast and caricatured. Those we meet in the second chapter are from a privileged class; educated, comparatively rich, they have accepted many of the benefits of western civilisation. They are, nevertheless, dissatisfied with their lot; aware of etiquette and the rules of correct social behaviour, they are vulnerable by the very fact of their having absorbed European sophistication; they are thus constantly humiliated by the Anglo-Indians. But in them Forster appears to confirm feckless tendencies, which were at the time frequently attributed to Indians: they take the word for the deed; their reason is subjected to their emotions; they are incapable of punctuality; they cheat and lie charmingly and they skilfully hide their resentments from their British rulers. Mahmoud Ali's extravagances at the trial match those of Major Callendar, move for move, whilst the punkah-wallah's oblivion to all that goes on around him adds an extra dimension of unreality to the proceedings. Left to their own devices, as in Mau, the Indians neglect education and turn their High School into a grain store; even Aziz allows his surgical instruments to rust and runs the hospital 'at half-steam' (Chapter 34).

These two groups have little in common, except that they share the same land and the same sky. We repeatedly see, however, the high-handedness of the conquerors and the servility of the dominated: the arrogant assumption that the Indians have no social life leads Major Callendar to show his power by calling Aziz away from Hamidullah's dinner-party; the egocentricity of the women folk allows them to appropriate Aziz's tonga;

the condescension of the Anglo-Indians at the Bridge Party precludes any possibility of breaking down barriers. After the fiasco of the trial the defiance of the Indians is of the kind practised by inferiors against their superiors. Yet Forster extracts no obvious political message from the general circumstances of the two groups, teaches no lessons, reaches no conclusions. He presents the evidence and leaves us to draw our own inferences. That something is wrong in the administration of Anglo-India we are left in no doubt but of the steps needed to put it right we cannot be sure.

The principal characters – Mrs Moore, Adela, Fielding and Aziz – only partially underline the racial conflict, for although Adela and Aziz are the main antagonists, the sympathies of Mrs Moore and Fielding lie more with Aziz than with their own compatriots. Similarly, Aziz's determined assertion of affinity with Mrs Moore again crosses racial barriers. Thus Forster retreats from the larger political issues to consider individuals and their relationships.

3.3 THE PRINCIPAL THEME: PERSONAL RELATIONS

'Only connect', the epigraph to *Howards End* (1910), embodies the principal theme of all Forster's novels. He is not concerned, as Conrad is, with Man's anguish at his own isolation but rather with the unseen barriers that divide man from man, class from class, race from race. The yearning of his characters is towards connection and understanding but all human experience appears to point towards the futility of any such hope. The early novels examine this problem in a comparatively straightforward way, seeking simple relationships between man and woman and through such relationships attempting to bridge the gap between class and class; they simultaneously examine the clashes which occur when art, culture and philistinism are thrown together. The European setting, however, is common to these novels and thus provides a background of common understanding and civilisation; marriage and friendship are at least possible, though only in *A Room With a View* and *Maurice* do we feel that connections have been successfully made.

A Passage to India removes us from our own familiar world to a setting that is at once exotic, strange and disturbing. An extra dimension is introduced into the story through its colonial aspect. Two civilisations are seen, existing side by side, but it is decreed that never the twain shall meet. The Indians, despite their position as a subjugated nation, have their own rigid class system, in which the wealthy, the educated and the 'westernised' are seen to be poles part from the poor and the ignorant. Furthermore, they are divided too by a multiplicity of languages and religions at odds with each other, a nation that cannot see its way to healing the rifts between its own peoples. The distinctions between the Anglo-Indians are perhaps less apparent because their role in India dictates that they come in general from the fairly narrow band of the British upper-middle class. However, at any moment when the opposing class systems touch, the most superior of the Indians is declared to be no more than equal with the least of their English rulers; as Mrs Turton emphasises in her words to Mrs Moore and Adela Quested at the Bridge Party: 'You're superior to everyone in India except one or two of the ranis, and they're on an equality' (Chapter 5).

It is against this background that Forster appears to reappraise his view of relationships. For Helen and Margaret Schlegel in *Howards End* personal relations are supreme, 'the real life, for ever and ever' (Chaper 4); the relationships that work in the novel are based on compromise, on each side moving in some measure towards the point of view of the other, not on defiance or rebellion, nor on the complete abandonment of an established position. To some extent, *A Passage to India* continues this trend, for issues are not stated in clear terms of black or white; if connections are to be made, both sides must shift their ground. Thus, even within the Anglo-Indian community, it is apparent to us that marriage between Adela and Ronny can never work. Their coming together is based merely on the animality of sensual desire; Ronny has not shifted his ground one fraction of a millimetre and Adela has not considered realistically the adjustments she will have to make in her own conscience to embrace her fiancé's view of India. What hope is there then of the much broader understandings necessary before harmony on an international scale becomes possible?

Deliberately imposed solutions to the problem are shown not to work, for friendship cannot be predetermined. The chance connection established between Mrs Moore and Aziz is the most enduring in the novel. It begins inauspiciously with Aziz attempting to set up the barrier of religion between them; yet Mrs Moore, with her own personal brand of Christian tolerance, brushes his doubts aside. She feels no compulsion to make a relationship succeed; she is, indeed, not concerned with relationships. In the mosque she accepts Aziz as a person without regard to sex or age or race or creed. Later in the novel, on the journey to the Marabar Caves, she is to reflect that 'though people are important, the relations between them are not' (Chapter 14). Forster has travelled beyond the belief in personal relationships, so strongly expressed in *Howards End* to a belief in the value of the individual. People matter intrinsically, not as appendages of others. Forster's Anglo-Indians need to learn not to despise, perhaps not even to understand, but to accept; on the other hand, Mrs Moore, Fielding and Aziz are alike in their readiness to accept others without reference to the conditions that divide, communing directly, heart to heart, and thus overcoming the barriers that attempt to impose unequal measures. By the end of the novel, though Mrs Moore is dead and Fielding and Aziz have to part, connections have been made. The love between a young Indian doctor and an old Englishwoman is to endure out of time and beyond death: '. . .she had stolen to the depths of his heart, and he always adored her' (Chapter 36); it outstrips the usual concept of relationship. The affectionate understanding between Fielding and Aziz, whilst it does not become a present reality, prepares the ground for universal goodwill when English and Indians can be friends without reservation; through the persons of the main protagonists East and West have moved a step nearer to each other; the words 'yet' and 'there' in the final sentence qualify the apparent negations and offer hope for the future.

The novel transcends Forster's own liberal humanism in its uneasy dalliance with the supernatural and this aspect will be dealt with below.

3.4 THE MYSTIC ELEMENT

Religion in its widest sense is both more and less than a theme in *A Passage to India*: it permeates the whole fabric of the book, yet Forster has not written a religious novel. The title is taken from the poem 'Passage to India' by the American poet, Walt Whitman (1819-92), a poem concerned, not with physical journeyings, but with the voyage of the soul:

> Passage to more than India!
> Are thy winds plumed indeed for such far flights?
> O soul, voyagest thou indeed on voyages like those?
> Disportest thou on waters such as those?
> . . .
> . . .
> . . .
> O my brave soul!
> O farther, farther sail!
> O daring joy, but safe! are they not all the seas of God?
> O farther, farther, farther sail!

Although Mrs Moore and Adela Quested have taken their 'passage to India' their real experiences lie, not in their actual physical explorations, but in the realms of the spirit. Yet their discoveries are not informed by the beliefs of any particular religion; several, indeed, are examined and, in some respects at least, found wanting.

The first part 'Mosque' and the third part 'Temple' focus on the two principal Indian religions, Mohammedanism and Hinduism, represented respectively by Aziz and Godbole; Mrs Moore, on the other hand, becomes a spokeswoman for Western religion, loosely based on the main precept of

Christianity, 'God is love', the words of St John the Apostle (I John 4.16). Of these three, however, only Hinduism, itself a mystic religion to Western understanding, is presented in its full dress, with the ceremony of the Birth of Krishna dominating the action of Part III.

Neither Aziz nor Mrs Moore seek comfort in the formalities of their religion, nor do they appear to be especially devout. Aziz sees Islam as 'an attitude towards life both exquisite and durable' (Chapter 2); imaginatively and emotionally it fulfils a need in him which he tries to articulate through poetry. Mrs Moore has accepted certain tenets of the Christian faith based on love and understanding but God Himself continues to elude her; she knows no greater name to call on, yet the feeling that she lacks a sure response troubles her (Chapter 5). Such problems do not trouble Godbole; as he explains, 'I say to Him, Come, come, come, come, come, come. He neglects to come' (Chapter 7) but if he yearns to reach beyond his grasp he nevertheless accepts his own shortcomings; what he achieves through love may be inadequate, yet he knows it is more than he is himself (end of Chapter 34).

The spiritual quality of the novel, however, does not lie in its concern with specific religions; there is an indefinable mystic aura which pervades the action. Understatements and negations which suggest the existence of their opposites (compare the comment about 'yet' and 'there' in the previous section) are discernible from the beginning; when, for instance, Forster describes the city of Chandrapore in the opening chapter he comments that the Ganges 'happens not to be holy here', a clear acceptance that elsewhere the Ganges is 'holy', that the concept of 'holiness' has reality. Likewise, later on when the Sunday church bells ring out, those from the Civil Station ring out boldly, implying a partisanship with the master-race of Anglo-Indians, whilst – we are told – the bells from the mission station ring out 'feebly to mankind' (Chapter 8). Yet, however, feeble the summons, their call is universal and acknowledges the possibility of spiritual unity.

No recognisable and systematised pattern of belief can be constructed from the many references in the novel to God, to good and evil, to heaven, to an afterlife but they all contribute to the strong mystic element which is present; this element is mainly vested in Mrs Moore who exerts an almost inexplicable spiritual influence upon those with whom she comes into contact. Her single-minded approach to the problems of race, colour and creed is prompted by humanitarian beliefs, often couched in religious terms. When she tells Aziz in the mosque that 'God is here' it is more a recognition of the susceptibilities of her fellow men than an acknowledgement of the presence of God. Her words to Ronny in Chapter 5 are unequivocally based on a gospel of universal love: 'God...is...love... The desire to behave pleasantly satisfies God...Though I speak with the tongues of. . .' Although the quotation remains unfinished, we should recall its biblical context: 'Though I speak with the tongues of men and of angels, and have not charity [that is, love]. . .it profiteth me nothing' (I Corinthians 13.1-3). Love governs her actions and enables her to reach out towards universal brotherhood and the beliefs by which she lives transcend mortality so that, when she is dead, her spirit remains, linking together Moslem, Hindu and Christian in a brotherhood of love.

The deification of Mrs Moore's name, first at Chandrapore during the trial and later by the Hindus in the Gokul Ashtami ceremony, not only suggests to us that a myth has been born but also shows us the spiritually receptive state of the Moslem Aziz in Hindu Mau. 'Esmiss Esmoor' represents for him the 'syllables of salvation'; though he accepts rationally that 'She had not borne witness in his favour, nor visited him in the prison' (Chapter 36), he knows that witness was silently borne through Mrs Moore's influence upon Adela and that, though she had not visited him, Mrs Moore had assuredly saved him from prison.

Throughout the novel Mrs Moore is more aware than the other characters of the spirit world. She appears to be attuned to an extra-human wavelength which brings the supernatural within her range of perception. Her introduction to us is highly emotive: as Aziz sits in the mosque, dreaming sentimentally about death and poetry, he sees pillar after pillar seemingly quiver and sway so that his thoughts turn to ghosts; his 'ghost', however, is Mrs Moore, quietly making her way out of the mosque. Later, the less imaginative Adela is to feel that Mrs Moore, in her meeting with Aziz, has glimpsed the real spirit of India (Chapter 5). The ghostly world becomes a minor theme, insubstantial as is no doubt appropriate, but weaving an uncertain pattern through the web of the novel and repeatedly linked with the idea of telepathy. It is Mrs Moore who hardly mentions, who no more than breathes the thought that the Nawab Bahadur's car had been attacked by a ghost when he drove with Adela and Ronny along the Marabar road; yet, at the very moment of her thought, the Nawab himself is remembering how nine years previously he had run over a drunk man and killed him on that very road. But, we are told, 'None of the English people knew of this, nor did the chauffeur; it was a racial secret communicable more by blood than speech' (Chapter 8). Later, Mrs Moore is to convey to Adela, without speech, her conviction that Aziz is innocent and later still Adela is to suggest to Fielding that Mrs Moore knew, by telepathy, what had occurred in the cave, that there were, perhaps, 'worlds beyond' their consciousness (Chapter 29).

The word 'telepathy' was coined by F. W. H. Myers in 1882 at the founding meeting of the Society for Psychical Research and during the years that followed there was considerable controversy about the truth of psychical phenomena. During the years 1910-24 Professor Gilbert Murray

and his family carried out an exhaustive series of experiments on pure telepathy, the results of which were published in the *Proceedings of the Society
for Psychical Research*, Volume XXIX. Much of this research coincided
with the long period of gestation of *A Passage to India* which was probably
begun in 1913; it seems unlikely that Forster was not aware of the current
interest and the arguments surrounding it, particularly as the Cambridge of
his own university days was a centre for such research.

The problem of the survival of human personality was, likewise, a subject which much exercised the minds of the psychical researchers at this
time and this too was a theme which Forster employed. His first sustained
use of the idea is in *Howards End* where Mrs Wilcox dies between the end
of Chapter 8 and the beginning of Chapter 9, yet remains to influence the
action till the end. Here, in *A Passage to India*, Mrs Moore dies far away
from Chandrapore, a bodily death which releases her spirit to live again at
the trial, to become a Hindu goddess, to sway Adela's mind and to change
the course of justice. Twice Aziz feels her presence though he believes her
to be far away and when, in fact, she is no longer alive; later, when Fielding
tries to convince him that she is indeed dead, Fielding finds himself,
though a 'frank atheist' teased by uncertainty: 'He had tried to kill Mrs
Moore this evening on the roof of the Nawab Bahadur's house; but she still
eluded him' (end of Chapter 27). The reader too is left in doubt about the
significance of the supernatural in this novel: 'Perhaps life is', after all, 'a
mystery, not a muddle' (Chaper 29).

3.5 THE PROBLEM OF NATIONHOOD

'India a nation! What an apotheosis!' Fielding's mocking words to Aziz at
the end of the novel voice doubts which have been repeatedly hinted at
earlier; the rifts apparent within native India are shown to be as great as
the barriers which divide English and Indian. *A Passage to India* is concerned mainly with the Moslem population of Chandrapore, though Hindus
live and work there freely: Professor Godbole teaches in Government
College; Dr Panna Lal works with Aziz at the hospital; Mr Das is a magistrate; Mr Bhattacharya runs a monthly magazine.

Even among the educated and professional people there is friction. Aziz
frequently manifests anti-Hindu propensities: he deliberately picks a
quarrel with his colleague Dr Lal and later describes him to Mrs Moore as
'a slack unpunctual fellow'; he constantly connects Hindus with cow-dung;
when he is ill and is visited by his Moslem friends they learn that Godbole
is also ill and, without justification, begin to slander Hindus in general,
speaking of them with disgust. In view of this it is not surprising that
troubles arise over the Mohurram procession, with both Moslems and
Hindus provoking each other.

At Mau, however, Aziz settles happily to life in a Hindu state and for all practical purposes lives as a Hindu and is 'chief medicine man to the court'. Though nominally subject to British rule Mau has no resident British officials and scarcely any Moslem inhabitants; the difference between life in Anglo-Indian Chandrapore and Hindu Mau is the significant lack of arrogance and oppression.

Yet Forster makes it clear that the obstacles to a united India are more subtle than merely the religious differences. The life of Aziz and his friends is not dissimilar from the life of the Anglo-Indians, though materially on a lower scale; they dress in western clothes, they are educated, they have a social life and they can discuss poetry and philosophy. Other Indians, in the same land, wear only a loincloth, or go naked and spend their lives in abject worship of a 'scarlet doll'. Language too divides, even those of the same religion; so, as Mr Syed Mohammed gets excited while talking to his friends, he lapses into his native Punjabi and becomes unintelligible. Their eating habits prevent Hindus, Moslems and Christians from enjoying social meals together for there are taboos on beef, on ham, on eggs, on alcohol, which greatly inhibit the choice of foods; thus on the Marabar expedition Aziz's worries about food for his guests are blamed on him because he has not accepted the prevailing spirit of India which tries to keep men separate. Furthermore, Moslem women are kept in purdah, apart from all men except those of their own family.

Wherever we look there are divisions and discord. In the hot weather 'a barrier of fire' separates the mountainous north of the country from the great central plain and the sea. During the rains the rivers overflow and cut off communication. The very land is full of fissures and rocky outcrops which force men to pass along in single file.

It is a sign of the balance and restraint of Forster's picture of India that he does not leave us with the feeling that, but for English domination, India could establish itself as a nation. Writing the novel in the early 1920s he was under no illusions about the possibilities of Indian unity. Aziz may dream of a motherland (Chapter 30), of being 'an Indian at last' (Chapter 34), but in the end he is no more convinced than we are that nationhood is possible. The civil war and the partition of 1947 which followed confirm this view, though when he published *The Hill of Devi* in 1953 Forster was clearly not happy with the solutions brought about at that time. He wanted ' "India"... to designate the whole sub-continent' and he went on to say:

> Much as I sympathise with the present government at New Delhi I wish it had not chosen 'India' to describe its territory. Politicians are too prone to plunder the past.

'Nationhood' received its death-blow in 1947.

4 TECHNIQUES

4.1 NARRATION AND POINT OF VIEW

The narrative method of *A Passage to India* is neither innovative nor complicated. It employs a third person omniscient narrator who is, for the most part, completely non-intrusive; at only one point in the novel does Forster step into the story, acknowledge its novelistic character and, in Dickensian style, address his 'dear reader' (Chapter 23). For the rest, a discreet anonymity is observed.

The plot is unfolded chronologically, though explanations are sometimes given after the event, rather than before; so we learn that the Nawab Bahadur had once run over and killed a drunk man only after the motor accident and his display of fear; again, Aziz is arrested before we learn what crime he is accused of. Yet neither of these incidents may be seen as a deliberate stylistic inversion of the order of events for, in the first instance the Nawab Bahadur has deliberately suppressed his unpleasant memories, whilst in the second the narrative has remained with Aziz and his party who are ignorant of Adela's accusations.

The action of the novel is introduced by and interspersed with sustained descriptive passages and philosophic discussions. The plot progresses through a series of incidents centring on groups or individuals as they react with each other. Our sympathies are engaged with some characters and not with others by the simple device of allowing us to view some from outside and others from inside.

The principal characters are seen in varying lights; what they do and what happens to them is put into focus by an insight into their reasons for action and their reactions to events. Furthermore, they appear to have a life apart from the plot of the novel, as they muse on poetry, religion, philosophy and other subjects which affect and reflect their innermost thoughts; it is from their point of view that we comprehend the tensions of the action. When, for instance, in Chapter 2, Aziz is called to report to

Major Callendar, we are immediately aware of the lack of civility in the Civil Surgeon's note and we feel the young doctor's humiliation when Mrs Lesley and Mrs Callendar slight him. This incident, though ostensibly told by an omniscient narrator, is seen through Aziz's eyes and the reader becomes sympathetically involved with him. Conversely, there is no attempt to let us understand the point of view of Callendar and the womenfolk and we thus remain opposed to them.

The narrator does not often describe characters, rarely refers to what they are wearing and never directly tells us what to think about them or the action they are involved in. In so far as our sympathies are manipulated, they are so through the characters themselves. This, however, is a fairly traditional method of narration and has been used in the conventional novel, certainly from Jane Austen onward.

4.2 CHARACTERS AND CHARACTERISATION

Forster's named characters are given to us not merely against the setting of India but also against a background of the vast unnamed population, the circles beyond circles of the inhabitants of India, 'humanity grading and drifting beyond the educated vision' (Chapter 4). The Westernised Indians who live and work in the vicinity of the British Civil Station are but a small and atypical proportion of the native people; they are those who aspire to a more advanced mode of life, who look for personal fulfilment in the Western professions such as medicine, teaching and law, who believe that they may achieve nationhood for India.

Forster is not strong on characterisation. His main interest is in ideas rather than people. He does not illustrate and develop the qualities of his characters but rather presents them in relation to his theme and their emotional responses to it. This is not to say that they lack realism, for his principal protagonists are real enough with regard to the situation of the novel; they feel and think but we do not easily envisage them in other situations. For instance, Mrs Moore lives for us only in India; we cannot imagine her life in England and, significantly, she dies as she leaves Bombay.

Aziz

Aziz is the main protagonist of the novel and the only Indian treated in any depth. We know little about his physical appearance, except that he is about five foot nine inches tall, athletic and slimly built; he generally dresses in Western clothes, mainly to avoid being picked on by the police. He is a doctor at the hospital in Chandrapore, working under Major Callendar, the Civil Surgeon; Aziz himself is a gifted and skilful surgeon, fascinated by modern medical progress, and he practises his profession with enthusiasm. Yet, though his mind has embraced the wonders of Western science, he is still emotionally attached to the culture and traditions of his own country and of his Islamic religion.

The plot of the novel begins with Aziz as he arrives late for Hamidullah's dinner party and impulsively drops his bicycle down before a servant can catch it. Unpunctuality is an Indian shortcoming of which he is well aware, yet it is not within his nature to arrive on time: in order not to be late for the Marabar expedition he goes to the other extreme, camping overnight with the servants at the station. Lateness signifies little in Indian life and it is immediately apparent in the opening incident that no one thinks less of Aziz because he is always late and his apology is passed off jokingly. His impulsiveness and exuberance are, however, personal traits of considerable significance as the plot progresses.

We see him first among his own friends, happy, at ease, content to listen to an argument between Hamidullah and Mahmoud Ali about the English; his lack of involvement is shown by his only contribution to the discussion, which is to wonder whether it is necessary to make the commitment of being friends or 'not friends' at all. When they join his host's wife behind the purdah we learn a little of Aziz's domestic circumstances. His wife is dead and his children – two boys and a girl – live with their maternal grandmother, whilst he lives poorly in Chandrapore, sending away all his salary to support them. The stock Indian solution to this problem would be to take another wife but Aziz is Westernised enough not to wish to marry a woman chosen for him by others and Oriental enough to know that if he is to marry again there is little alternative. By the third part of the novel he has pushed aside his aspirations towards Western life and, living and working among the Hindus, he has remarried and brought his children to live with him.

Our first view of Aziz, the private man, is swiftly overlaid by a view of him not only as professional man but also as a member of a subject race. With his Indian friends he can laugh and joke as an equal but as Major Callendar's subordinate he has to obey orders; furthermore, as an Indian he has to suffer humiliation without redress at the hands of the Anglo-Indians.

When he meets Mrs Moore in the mosque he takes on yet another role; his attempt to bully her gives way to an open, natural, friendly communion, untainted by thoughts of race, religion or sex. Though he is not at the time aware of it, this is one of the most significant moments of his life for the meeting is one of hearts, not of minds, and the emotional tie he establishes remains with him even after Mrs Moore's death. Later, during the Krishna Festival he finds himself alone with Ralph Moore and against his will he is overcome by feelings of love and friendship, his heart 'too full to draw back' (Chapter 36).

The impulsiveness which attaches him to Mrs Moore is accompanied by a deep, perhaps almost subconscious, desire to establish connections with the English, to get beneath superficialities which separate to find the spirit which unites. His route to such unity is not through the intellect but through the heart, as he searches for 'some truth of religion or love'. Though his mind is engaged with his profession, he is at heart a dreamer, a poet; cultured, he is well-versed in the history of his country, he has a knowledge of art and reads Persian. At Mau he returns to writing poetry which he had felt unable to do in Chandrapore.

Despite his learning, Aziz lacks the ability to bring logic to bear upon his problems; his response is always instinctive rather than rational. Thus, he rips out his collar-stud to give to Fielding, regardless of the fact that his own collar will rise up; or again, at a moment's whim, having let down his colleague Dr Panna Lal at the Bridge Party, he reinforces enmity between them by deliberately frightening Dr Lal's horse. More seriously, however, when Adela disappears on the Marabar expedition, Aziz invents a story which allows him to save face and the telling of it makes him believe it is true. Practically everything he does at this time incriminates him in Western eyes; it is only through Fielding's intervention that he does not run away when McBryde arrests him at the station; such an act would have immediately confirmed his guilt to the Anglo-Indians, his emotional reaction appearing to them incomprehensible.

After the trial the harsher side of Aziz's nature comes to the fore; his attitude towards Anglo-India hardens; he refuses to recognise Adela's courage and shows a lack of generosity towards her; he convinces himself of Fielding's perfidy and deliberately breaks his ties with the Englishman. Finally, in Mau, free of the pressures of Anglo-India, he is able to reassemble his life; he is less subservient, more realistic. His sentimental affection for Mrs Moore, however, remains and is transferred to her son Ralph. Yet Aziz knows that the time is not ripe for friendship between the two races and the novel ends with his acceptance of the inevitability of separation between him and Fielding.

The character of Aziz was partly based on that of Forster's Moslem friend Syed Ross Masood (see page 3) to whom *A Passage to India* is dedicated. He has, too, affinities with characters in earlier novels, such as Gino in *Where Angels Fear To Tread* (1905) or Stephen Wonham in *The Longest Journey* (1907); in this final novel, however, Aziz is depicted as more thoughtful, more artistic, more philosophic than his predecessors.

Mrs Moore

Mrs Moore is the most enigmatic of all the characters in *A Passage to India.* An elderly Englishwoman, she, like Aziz, has her precursors in Forster's work, most particularly in Mrs Wilcox of *Howards End* (1910).

We see Mrs Moore at her best in the scene in the mosque with Aziz. There she is considerate and sympathetic, light-hearted and completely frank. Despite his initial roughness, she treats Aziz with easy friendship and as an equal. Her understanding and tolerance are apparent in her acceptance of God's presence in the mosque. The words 'God is here' are a significant indication of her spirituality; when, later, she argues with Ronny about the duties of the English in India she returns to the subject of God's omnipresence, emphasising her belief that God's will is that man shall love his neighbour.

Her visit to India brings about a crisis in Mrs Moore's spiritual life. Ronny believes that her religious bouts are always a sign of ill-health; certainly she is tired and dispirited for most of the time and we do not often see the side of her character which so endears her to Aziz. Her second meeting with Aziz at Fielding's tea party is the last time we see her in a carefree mood. Her problems begin at that party: first, Adela indiscreetly tells Aziz that she does not intend to settle in India; this remark indicates to Mrs Moore that her mission has resulted in failure and Fielding observes that she 'looked flustered and put out'; secondly, Ronny rudely breaks up the party and she realises that the English have no intention of being pleasant to the Indians, whether God is watching them or not; and thirdly, Professor Godbole's song suggests the possibility of the absence of God, that He is perhaps not, after all, omnipresent: 'I say to Him, Come, come, come, come, come, come. He neglects to come'. The song with its negative conclusion is followed by an almost mystic moment of silence:

> Ronny's steps had died away, and there was a moment of absolute silence. No ripple disturbed the water, no leaf stirred.

The absence of God is suggested by the reference to the water, for it recalls the biblical story of the troubling of the waters of Bethesda in which the movement of the water indicated the presence of an angel (St John 5.1-9).

From this time Mrs Moore is a changed person; on the way back from Fielding's she is querulous and refuses to go to watch the polo; she appears to be both physically and spiritually sick, out of tune with the life around her. Though the day ends with Adela and Ronny's engagement, she does not recover her enthusiasm for life. During the fortnight between the tea party and the Marabar expedition little happens to revive her spirits and on the journey to the caves there is again a palpable silence which seems to deny all purpose in life. It is inside the first cave, however, that Mrs Moore's breakdown occurs, when the silence becomes filled with meaningless echoes; she gives way to despair, rejecting 'poor, little talkative Christianity', finding her life empty of understanding, of affection, of all interest. An elderly woman, she is fatigued with the journey, has probably had too much sun and is suffering from the strains and stresses of her Indian visit;

she is, of course, physically ill and this manifests itself in mental and spiritual sickness. Before the trial she tries to free herself of the burdens of duty and responsibility but she is too distraught to do more than assert Aziz's innocence and thus sow the seeds of doubt in Adela's mind.

Though she becomes a cantankerous old woman, Mrs Moore never entirely loses the reader's sympathy. That she does not bear witness in the court for Aziz can hardly be held against her, for by that point she is a dying woman. It may also be said that she does, in fact, bear more powerful witness than her bodily presence could have done; she had no evidence on his behalf, only her acute knowledge of human character, but in spirit she is with Adela, maintaining his innocence; she is constantly alluded to during the trial scene and it is just after the invocation of 'Esmiss Esmoor' that Adela speaks 'more naturally and healthily than usual'.

After her death, Mrs Moore gains new significance. Does Forster intend us to believe that in the mystery of India part of her personality survives – to influence Adela, to fill Aziz with happiness, to be worshipped by the Hindus? There is no suggestion that she lives again in a Christian sense but that she has an extra-human awareness is evidenced again and again (see pp. 50-2).

Adela Quested

Adela Quested is a very ordinary upper-middle-class English girl. Not especially attractive, she is sensible and thoughful; her reactions to life in India are probably those of any reasonable, well-disposed visitor from the West. She is, however, a rather special visitor, for she has come to explore the possibilities of marrying and settling down as the wife of a British official in the country. Her expectations are, perhaps not surprisingly, confused; though the members of the Civil Club have reproduced a version of suburban England in Chandrapore, Adela has difficulty in understanding that the native population is excluded from this life, that English and Indians do not meet socially, that she is superior, the natives inferior. Like Mrs Moore she rejects the arrogance of the rulers but she recognises the fear that she may herself become like them if she stays in India. Her instinct to return home (expressed at Fielding's tea party) is sound, for Ronny has already absorbed the prevailing Anglo-Indian attitudes and he annoys and irritates her. The reader never quite believes in the possibility of the marriage. Perhaps Adela's feeling all along has been for Mrs Moore rather than for her son; she has a very real affection for Mrs Moore which is shown through her kindness and consideration for the older woman.

Adela's wish to see the 'real India' is accompanied by a genuine desire to make connections with the Indians but she does not know how to start. She seems to have no small talk and little lightness of heart; whilst Aziz and Mrs Moore can laugh together, Adela is always serious; Fielding describes her as 'a prig. . .trying ever so hard to understand India and life' (Chapter 11); her efforts to understand lead to the catastrophe in the cave. Just before they go into the first cave Adela expresses her concern to Aziz that in marrying Ronny she will become an Anglo-Indian and, in pursuing this conversation she touches him on a raw spot. On their way to the next cave she is suddenly overcome by the realisation that she does not love Ronny, that she is about to enter into a marriage without love; it is this reflection which prompts her to question Aziz about his marriage and to commit an even greater social blunder by asking him if he has more than one wife. She is unaware of her gaffe but, with her thoughts revolving round ideas of love and marriage, she enters the cave and appears to have an hallucination which is followed by some sort of emotional breakdown. Mrs Moore had suffered similarly and Aziz too panics in the vicinity of the caves, becoming disorientated and striking the guide.

At the trial, Adela's sense of honesty, fair play and decency finally triumphs and she comes out of it well, certainly better than Ronny, who deserts her in her hour of need. Her parting from Fielding in Chapter 29 shows her once more to have regained her balance; she is again logical and sensible but more subdued than on her arrival in India. She returns to England alone, having failed to make any real connections in India and having lost through Mrs Moore's death a relationship she treasured.

Fielding

Fielding, though not Forster himself, is generally assumed to represent Forster's point of view in this novel. Forty-five years old, he is exactly the age Forster was in 1924 when *A Passage to India* was first published. An easy-going, kindly man, he has stepped aside from the politics of conquest and rejected the role of 'sahib' with all its connotations of superiority. As Principal of Government College he necessarily mixes with Indians and, like the missionaries, is despised for encouraging them to advance themselves.

On his first appearance in the novel he advises Adela and Mrs Moore to 'try seeing Indians' if they want to get to know India; by this he means meeting with them, rather than viewing them from a distance. To this end he arranges his tea party to entertain the visiting Englishwomen and to bring them into contact with two of the educated Indians, Aziz and Godbole. Imbued with Forster's own liberal humanism he, like Mrs Moore, is not concerned with colour, race or creed. When he says to Aziz, 'Please make yourself at home' (Chapter 7), it is the kind of remark he would have made to any visitor; Aziz thinks it unconventional, which in an Anglo-Indian context it is, but he is nevertheless delighted.

Fielding is more at home with Indians than with Englishmen of the ruling class. He rarely goes to the Club except to play tennis or billiards and when he resigns he expects to miss no one except McBryde. Among the Indians, however, he is able to be himself. The parents of his pupils like him and he finds the company of the educated Indians congenial. His needs are simple; he wants friendship but he has little sexual desire.

A quality in Fielding which Aziz sees as both endearing and worrying is his outspokenness; at the Club he had offended his compatriots by a joke describing the 'so-called white races' as 'really pinko-gray' (Chapter 7); on his visit to Aziz's sick-bed he scandalises the Indians by renouncing belief in God; just before the trial he insists that Aziz is innocent, first at the meeting of the Civil Club and afterwards in a letter to Adela. He worries little as long as he speaks the truth as he sees it and he does not speak in rancour. Whilst Mrs Moore's kindness stems from her religious belief, however, Fielding's is an entirely human attribute; he is 'a holy man minus the holiness' (Chapter 11), travelling light because personal possessions have no appeal for him. Yet he too becomes involved in the catastrophe of the caves; against his will he is forced to take sides and he plumps for what he believes is the side of the wronged and oppressed, throwing in his lot with Aziz and his Indian friends. It is typical of him that after the fiasco of the trial he is the only Englishman to show any magnanimity towards Adela, even though it proves to be detrimental to the budding friendship between him and Aziz. His natural sympathy for the underdog is combined with a grudging admiration for the honesty which made her speak out in court. At the same time he is aware of the very Englishness of his gallantry and of the fact that if his Indian friends attacked Adela 'he would be obliged to die in her defence'.

At the end of Part II Fielding returns home and feels enlivened and revivified by the beauty of form of Italian buildings. A hint of his forthcoming marriage is contained in the last sentence of Chapter 32 when, arriving in England, 'tender romantic fancies' are reborn in him at the sight of the wild flowers of the countryside.

Two years later he returns to India; now married, he is harder, sterner, travelling less lightly than before. Love, which he had earlier felt no need of is passionate within him and Stella has the first place in his affection. He takes life more seriously, has more responsibilities and his profession has become more important to him financially. He is, too, less easy with Aziz and more ready to criticise him. The rift between them which came about after the trial is finally healed but the desire for friendship is out of tune with the time and place and he accepts the limitations imposed.

Professor Godbole

Godbole is a Hindu teacher at Government College where Fielding is Principal. He is one of the few characters described in detail to us; physically he looks rather like a European with his fair complexion, grey-blue eyes and grey moustache; he dresses in European clothes except for his turban and, remarks Forster, 'his whole appearance suggest[s] harmony' (Chapter 7). Apart from this, we know so little about him that we do not even know what he teaches and when he becomes Minister of Education at Mau he shows no real concern for education, allowing the King-Emperor George Fifth High School to be turned into a granary. A Brahman, a member of a superior social caste, he remains outside and above all the turmoil which surrounds the inhabitants of Chandrapore, English and Indian. He lives in the College where he teaches and does not appear to have, or to need, any social life outside his job and his religion.

He is not a very strict Hindu; nevertheless, he is always placed in a Hindu context: Aziz worries about the picnic at the Marabar because Godbole will not eat meat or anything that has eggs in it and will not allow anyone else to eat beef in his presence; at Fielding's tea party he sings a religious song which carries its echoes of desire and yearning through the rest of the novel – the god will never come, however often men beg him to do so. In the third part of the novel Godbole takes on a more active religious role, leading one of the choirs that sings in honour of the Birth of Krishna, dancing to the glory of the god and helping in the naming ceremony.

Though he is the chief representative of Hinduism in the novel, Professor Godbole has little to do with the main plot. He constantly cuts himself off from the action and his responses bewilder those who come into contact with him. When the caves are discussed in Chapter 7 it is Godbole who proves to be 'extraordinary'. The simple, straightforward mind of Aziz can make no headway with him; questions are stonewalled, information withheld. What he knows he keeps to himself so that genuine communication with him is impossible. His secrecy is seemingly purposeless, his mind impenetrable. After the incident at the caves he shocks Fielding by asking if the expedition was successful, even though he knows of the catastrophe. Fielding values his opinion and wants his advice but realises how impossible it is to pin him down. When he asks if Aziz is innocent or guilty, Godbole engages him in a philosophic discussion about the nature of good and evil but draws no satisfactory conclusions. Later, at Mau, it appears that Godbole knows that Fielding has married Stella Moore, yet though he is aware of Aziz's misconception he has made no attempt to clarify the matter. Finally he slips out of the novel as silently as he slipped away from Chandrapore.

The Anglo-Indians

Though they are essentially caricatures rather than living people, the Anglo-Indians can be distinguished from each other. **Ronny** is the least exaggerated and may be thought of, perhaps, as a functional character, rather than as a caricature; it is necessary to the plot that Mrs Moore and Adela go to India with a purpose, not just as holidaymakers; they must become involved with the Anglo-Indians so that they are able to view the Civil Club from inside; conversely, the Anglo-Indians must have reasons for involving the two ladies in their expatriate life. Ronny is the reason. We see him as a rather feeble young man who has allowed his career to destroy his humanity. He is so impressed by the opinions of his superiors that he fails to have any real opinions of his own; he finally abandons Adela because marriage to her would end his career in India. After the trial he is transferred from Chandrapore, only to make way for 'young Milner', who is the new City Magistrate, but likely to be little different from Ronny himself.

Of the longer established Anglo-Indians **Turton** and **McBryde** are the most reasonable, **Callendar** the worst. Early in the novel the latter is seen arrogantly asserting his authority over Aziz whom he dislikes, partly because he suspects that the young Indian doctor's surgical skills are greater than his own. On the other hand, Adela sees Turton and McBryde as being, with Fielding, the only Englishmen who had shown any common politeness at the Bridge Party. As for the **Englishwomen**, they are wholly objectionable and thus a powerful contrast to Adela and Mrs Moore.

The very exaggeration of the presentation of the Anglo-Indians makes them more acceptable to the reader. Their faults are so gross that they become comic and their lack of realism allows Forster to treat them harshly without appearing to be unfair.

4.3 STYLE AND LANGUAGE

A Passage to India is a skilfully crafted novel both in its overall pattern and in the details of its language. Its tripartite form – Mosque, Caves, Temple – is reflected by trinities of groupings within the body of the novel: three settings, three seasons, three religions, three attempts to form bridges, three children for both Aziz and Mrs Moore, three Moslem friends (Aziz, Hamidullah and Mahmoud Ali), three English who cannot be considered as Anglo-Indian (Mrs Moore, Fielding and Adela). The subtle insistence on the idea of 'threesomeness' emphasises separation and connection; the three parts of the novel are separated from each other not only geographically but also emotionally, yet each part is repeatedly brought to life in each of the other parts. So Part I begins with the caves and ends by recalling Aziz's mosque; Part II begins with the caves, recalls the mosque and looks forward to Mau; Part III, though taking place in Mau, simultaneously looks back to the events, characters and ideas of the earlier parts.

The method of reference and cross-reference, of simultaneity within variety, results in a novel that is highly structured yet not confined, a novel that opens out, rather than closes in. Not only the ending but the novel itself may be seen as illustrating one of Forster's own precepts in Chapter 8 of *Aspects of the Novel*: 'Expansion. That is the idea the novelist must cling to. Not completion. Not rounding off but opening out.'

The most striking feature of the language of *A Passage to India* is its use of what Forster himself, again in Chapter 8 of *Aspects of the Novel*, has described as 'rhythm'. He rejects the word 'symbol' because he feels that symbols are inclined to take over a novel and deflect the reader from the novelist's main purpose; for him, any motif a novelist uses should sometimes mean everything and sometimes be forgotten and mean nothing. With these caveats about Forster's own ideas, let us look in more detail at his use of symbol, image, rhythm, call it what you will.

The caves are central both to the whole pattern of the novel and to the imagery. Round, hollow, empty, they are without adornment, without beauty, without religious significance. The sky dominates but the caves set the tone of the novel. In their nihilism they hint at a nihilism at the heart of the universe; even physically they resemble the empty dome of the sky reaching out to infinity; the flame of a match reflected within their shining polished walls, like the stars in the vault of the sky, illuminates nothing but itself; a sound made within one of the caves is infinitely echoed until it loses its own identity.

In *The Cave and the Mountain* Professor Wilfred Stone has shown how significant the circular pattern is in Forster's work. Here, in *A Passage to India*, the concept of circularity is present in the form of the novel, which constantly returns to previous starting points, in the caves themselves, in the snakes with their tails in their mouths, in the repeated references to circles within circles which touch every aspect of Indian life – nature itself, the social framework and the political set-up within the country. The vocabulary reinforces the idea with the repeated use of words such as 'dome. . .vault. . .circle. . .circumference. . .arch. . .globe. . .bubble. . .ball . . .cycle'. Basic to the circular image and to the caves is the echo – not merely auditory but visual and conceptual as well. It appears in the first chapter when the distance between earth and stars is echoed by the ever-widening circles of distance behind them and by the faint memory of the blue-tinted daytime sky.

The more usual echo of sound does not occur until the novel has progressed into the second part. By that time, however, the echo image is well established and confirmed by the methods of its musical equivalents (again, see Chapter 8 of *Aspects of the Novel*). A word or phrase apparently randomly used and abandoned is picked up later, dropped again and again occurs: Mrs Moore's wasp which is first seen at the end of Chapter 3 is reintroduced at the end of Chapter 4 in the passage about the missionaries;

it is then left behind, forgotten, until it is recalled together with Mrs Moore by Professor Godbole in Chapter 33. The subsequent references to bees leave us slightly uneasy; this variation on the theme opens the novel out at the end, connecting Mrs Moore with her son Ralph and again with Aziz in a mystic communion. Similarly, the phrase first used by Aziz to Mrs Moore in the mosque, 'Then you are an Oriental' is echoed later in Chapter 27, again by Aziz referring to Mrs Moore; it is recalled in Chapter 34 when Aziz uses it to Ralph Moore and it is finally used by Fielding to Aziz in the last chapter of the book; Aziz does not reply to Fielding's remark but the significance of this echo is not lost on him and it is underlined for us by the narrator's words, 'Something – not a sight but a sound – flitted past him'; what flits past is, of course, the memory of his first use of these words to Mrs Moore and it leads him to add an affectionate comment about her in his letter to Adela.

There is a multiplicity of such echoing phrases: Godbole's song with its yearning plea to the god who never comes; Mrs Moore's assertion that 'God is love'; the idea of 'Kindness, kindness and more kindness'; the smell of cow-dung connected with Hindus; jackals; friezes; ghosts; 'the real India'; 'Esmiss Esmoor'; the colour red; nothingness. Each can be traced as it wanders through the novel, accumulating references and building up a wealth of contextual significance. Delicately handled leitmotifs, they never stand firmly as symbols but they serve to enrich the whole fabric of the novel for the percipient reader, calling to mind the context of the earlier references to add subtle layers of meaning as the novel progresses. Try to investigate some of these yourself.

More firmly set up as images are the snakes, the owls and the kites. It should be remembered that, while for us in the West the snake is a symbol of evil, it is often in the east an object of veneration, to be feared, perhaps (are not Christians bidden to fear God?), but also to be worshipped. Hindus associate the snake or serpent with the god Siva and it is often prominent in their festivals; here, in the naming ceremony of the god Shri Krishna, a 'cobra of papier-mâché' appears suddenly on the red carpet, simultaneously with the appearance of the cradle of the infant god. In reading *A Passage to India*, then, we must rid ourselves of any prejudices connoting the snake with evil. Mrs Moore is warned by Aziz about the danger from snakes but snakes do not constitute the threat to her in India. Likewise, the deadly poisonous Russell's viper found crawling round a classroom in Government College is of less concern to Fielding than the monstrous accusation made against Aziz. Forster does not use the serpent as a religious symbol; it is neither evil nor good. Tail in mouth it reflects the circular pattern and the empty O it forms echoes the nothingness, the nihilism of the caves. Through it can be seen the contradictions of India, 'the serpent of eternity made of maggots' (Chapter 23).

Kites too, preying upon human disaster, are woven into the pattern of the book. Hovering over the Bridge Party, they are in their turn hovered over by a vulture, above which, like the reverberations of an echo, is the sky. At the caves a Brahminy kite is introduced in a similar context of echoes, reminding us that previous attempts to connect have failed. Yet, earlier, before the party leaves Chandrapore, kites are mentioned in the same sentence as the stationmaster and owls, so that our mind drifts back to the evening that Aziz first met Mrs Moore, when he heard owls and smelt the fragrance of flowers from the stationmaster's garden.

The actual echo which dominates Part II of the novel is another thread of the intricately woven pattern of the book, just as every repeated image or phrase becomes in turn part of the echo. It manifests itself first through its absence on the plains before the Marabar Hills, emptying life of its meaning because nothing has any consequence. In the cave a reversal occurs; there, the presence of an echo intimidates and takes away hope: life has consequence (in that sounds no longer lie dead) but it is still without meaning as the echo reduces everything to 'the same monotonous noise'. Long after the sound has died away the echo remains; it destroys Mrs Moore who feels that the props supporting her spiritual life have been withdrawn. It stays with Adela, haunting her with an indefinable malice; in the presence of Mrs Moore it becomes less threatening but returns with all its force just before the trial, perhaps at the moment of Mrs Moore's death. Not until she affirms Aziz's innocence does Adela's echo disappear; certainly in this context the echo has been entirely associated with evil. Later Fielding is to reflect that though the 'original sound may be harmless...the echo is always evil' (Chapter 31) but his thought progresses no further. The echo of the caves remains a strange phenomenon, adding to the mystic dimension of the novel.

Just as phrases and images flit through the pages, so matters of import in the plot are often referred to briefly, recalled and apparently forgotten until the event they have prepared us for occurs. For instance, the attentive reader should not be taken by surprise by Mrs Moore's death. At the very outset Aziz observes that she is old 'with a red face and white hair' (Chapter 2); a little later (Chapter 5) Ronny recognises the religious strain in his mother as a 'symptom of bad health'; she tires easily and needs to rest after visits such as that to Government College; in the train on the way to the caves she falls asleep and we are told that she is 'in rather low health' and after her experience in the cave she thinks, 'I am going to be ill'; later she mentions that she gets headaches and puffs when she walks. When we gather all these references together we realise that we have been given the picture of a rather sick elderly woman who is constantly trying to do more than her state of health makes possible. The 'brief episode of pain' she experiences as she approaches Bombay is the final warning; Mrs Moore's death follows soon after, though the trial intervenes before we learn of it.

In a similar way we are prepared to meet at Mau the characters who had been involved in the action at Chandrapore.

Another aspect of Forster's language that is of special interest is his use of quotation and allusion. Some quotations, such as the quatrain of Persian poetry quoted by Aziz in Chapter 3, are used principally to enrich the texture of the novel. The series of biblical quotations, however, serve to underline the spiritual content and, particularly in Part III, to universalise the religious mythology.

Prominence is given to the mystic side of Mrs Moore by subtly equating her with a god or Christ-figure. When in Chapter 22 she complains about being held up from her business, the strange use of the word 'business' at this point recalls Christ's words to his mother in St Luke 2.49 that he must be about His Father's business; Chapter 23 parallels her with the sorrowing God of Lamentations 1.12 as she thinks 'there is no sorrow like my sorrow'; during the trial, Adela remembers her sitting 'in the shadow of a great rock' (see Isaiah 32.2) and when Mahmoud Ali calls upon the Anglo-Indians to bring Mrs Moore into the court in order to 'save' Aziz it is ultimately her name that saves him. Certainly in Part III Aziz is to hear her name chanted by the Hindu worshippers and to interpret it as 'the syllables of salvation'. Yet this identification is not insisted upon. References to it again wander through the novel, are lost, picked up and dropped again. The very last mention of her in the book, however, is Aziz's '. . .the name that is very sacred in my mind, namely Mrs Moore'.

The Gokul Ashtami festival in Part III is given wider significance by being repeatedly referred to in biblical terms so that, whilst it retains its Hindu origin, it is also placed in a Christian context. The birth of Krishna is at one and the same time the birth of Christ; Gokul is Bethlehem, King Kansa is Herod and Krishna's salvation that of Christ.

Echoes of biblical stories tantalise the reader with doubts and memories: 'God so loved the world that he. . .' gave His only begotten Son (St John 3.16)? – No – '. . .that he took monkey's flesh upon him'. There are references to the 'Ark of the Lord' (see, for example, I Kings 2.26), to the 'Despised and Rejected' (see Isaiah 53.3); sorrow is annihilated (see Isaiah 35.10); the freeing of prisoners takes place. The hope brought to men by the Birth ceremony is thus for all men and, together with the abundant rains, it contains a promise for the future, again opening the novel out, expanding it rather than seeking completion.

Forster uses quite a number of specialised Anglo-Indian, Hindi or Arabic words in the novel. In many cases their meaning is self-evident or apparent from the context. The Penguin Modern Classics edition, however, contains a useful glossary of such words and should solve any difficulties.

In general, Forster's Indian characters speak excellent standard English. Aziz's grasp of idiom impresses Fielding in Chapter 7, though in Chapter 2 he twice uses the un-idiomatic 'in the same box' to Mrs Moore. When they talk among themselves Aziz and his friends would probably, in fact, speak Arabic but Forster has not fallen into the trap of translating this into a kind of 'pidgin English' to indicate that it is not their native language. Only Mohammed Latif speaks the English of the stage-Indian, such as 'You spick a lie' (Chapter 13) when Aziz teases him and this is at least partly because he is considered to be the comic turn of the Marabar expedition. Aziz himself speaks of his 'imperfect English' but his imperfections are hardly noticeable to the reader.

5 SPECIMEN PASSAGE AND COMMENTARY

This section is entirely devoted to a detailed critical examination of a passage from Chapter 4 of *A Passage to India*.

5.1 SPECIMEN PASSAGE

He had spoken in the little room near the Courts where the pleaders waited for clients; clients, waiting for pleaders, sat in the dust outside. These had not received a card from Mr Turton. And there were circles even beyond these – people who wore nothing but a loincloth, people who wore not even that, and spent their lives in knocking two sticks together before a scarlet doll – humanity grading and drifting beyond the educated vision, until no earthly invitation can embrace it.

All invitations must proceed from heaven perhaps; perhaps it is futile for men to initiate their own unity, they do but widen the gulfs between them by the attempt. So at all events thought old Mr Graysford and young Mr Sorley, the devoted missionaries who lived out beyond the slaughterhouses, always travelled third on the railways, and never came up to the club. In our Father's house are many mansions, they taught, and there alone will the incompatible multitudes of mankind be welcomed and soothed. Not one shall be turned away by the servants on that verandah, be he black or white, not one shall be kept standing who approaches with a loving heart. And why should the divine hospitality cease here? Consider, with all reverence, the monkeys. May there not be a mansion for the monkeys also? Old Mr Graysford said No, but young Mr Sorley, who was advanced, said Yes; he saw no reason why monkeys should not have their collateral share of bliss, and he had sympathetic discussions about them with his Hindu friends. And the jackals? Jackals were indeed less to Mr Sorley's mind, but he admitted that the mercy of God, being infinite, may well embrace all mammals. And the wasps? He became uneasy during the descent to wasps, and was apt to change the conversation. And oranges, cactuses, crystals and mud? and the bacteria inside Mr Sorley? No, no, this is going too far. We must exclude someone from our gathering, or we shall be left with nothing.

5.2 COMMENTARY

When Mr Turton issues invitations to the Bridge Party the Indians argue as to whether they should accept or not. The Nawab Bahadur settles the issue by himself deciding to go, for he sways opinion generally towards accept-ance. It is to his words that the opening sentence of this passage refers. As so often in this novel, however, the plot slips away; we find ourselves called upon to consider not the Anglo-Indian situation in Chandrapore but an aspect of India almost beyond an English person's comprehension and a religious philosophy which continually intrudes itself in different forms upon the action.

The novel is preoccupied with various aspects of religion, Christian, Moslem and Hindu. The first and last parts are named respectively for the place of worship of the Moslems and Hindus – 'Mosque' and 'Temple'. It is perhaps surprising that, apart from the missionaries, we are offered no view of the more formal practice of the Christian religion, for it is virtually certain that a chaplain would have conducted services at the Club, even if there was no Church building in Chandrapore. Again and again, however, we see that religion does not heal breaches but rather separates. Not only do the missionaries find themselves cut off from their compatriots but also Mrs Moore's very personal brand of Christianity separates her from her son Ronny who approves of religion but only 'as long as it endorse[s] the National Anthem'. Moslems and Hindus are constantly at odds with each other, their religion keeping them apart.

The themes of separation and exclusion prominent here are significant in the novel as a whole, for the social structure of Anglo-India makes any sort of personal relationship, except on rigid racial lines, virtually impos-sible. The Bridge Party is to take place in the garden of the Club, the nearest any Indian is likely to get to the sacrosanct premises. The Club is specifically a meeting place for white people and we have already learned from Aziz that Indians are not allowed inside, even as guests. Here we see the two missionaries deliberately excluding themselves because what they teach is at odds with the prevailing ethos of Anglo-India. Fielding, too, rarely goes there and just before the trial he is expelled, since his cham-pioning of Aziz's cause puts him outside the pale of what the Club sees as civilised behaviour; he is later reinstated by order of the Lieutenant-

Governor. These divisions, however, are as nothing compared with the fissures in Indian society; the teeming millions whom Mr Turton has not invited to the Bridge Party are as far removed from the educated Indians as they are from the English.

Two of the major images in the novel – the echo and the circle – are used as structural devices as well as images; both appear here, employed in the first instance to portray the vast, sprawling population of India. Throughout the novel there is constant emphasis on circularity – domes, lamps, round caves, globes, coils; even the boats that capsize in the Mau tank revolve 'like a mythical monster in the whirlwind'. Here the ever-expanding circles of Indians grade and drift outwards from the cultured Nawab and his friends to the naked, primitive idol-worshippers. Simultaneously, the circle motif is an echo-image; as the circles widen and widen they are like the reverberations of the echo which become less and less well defined.

The echo image is technically very skilful for, once employed, it is a part of every continuous image in the novel, echoing what has gone before. Thus, the wasps and the jackals recall a passage in the previous chapter; the jackals merely serve to reinforce the evocation of that earlier scene but the wasps are more significant. Young Mr Sorley finds himself unable to extend the mercy of God to the wasps – and this begins the series of exclusions from his heaven (echoing, incidentally, the exclusions discussed above). In Chapter 3, however, Mrs Moore had extended her love and tolerance to the wasp hanging on her peg. Later, in the Temple section, we are to see Professor Godbole strive to include in his love, first Mrs Moore and then a wasp, though he jibs at including the stone the wasp is sitting on. As this image accumulates in the novel it demonstrates the tolerance and spiritual love of Mrs Moore; unlike the missionaries and Godbole she settles for what is possible and does not strive to go beyond what is before her; she loves the wasp, just as she loves Aziz, because it is there.

Yet another echo relates this extract to the first chapter of Part III. There we meet with what Forster describes as 'the toiling ryot, whom some call the real India'. They are the Mau villagers for whom anything outside their village passes in a dream; they clearly have affinities with the 'humanity grading and drifting beyond the educated vision' of this passage. Just as here some of them spend their lives in apparently futile worship before a scarlet doll, so the people of Mau have gathered to celebrate the Birth of Krishna, who is represented by a 'red silk napkin' which is both God and not God.

Finally, the discussion of heaven should also remind us of a passage in the previous chapter when the Anglo-Indian women are talking with Mrs Moore and Adela Quested. Mrs Callendar, the Civil Surgeon's wife, suggests that the best thing to do for a sick Indian is to let him die; Mrs Moore intervenes with the sly reminder that dead Indians may go to heaven. One of the women, an ex-nurse, wants natives excluded from her heaven and explains that because of this she disapproves of missionaries. We can understand why Mr Graysford and Mr Sorley do not go to the Club, for they express the belief that God will receive all who come to Him in love, whatever the colour of their skin. Mrs Moore echoes this idea later, when she insists to Ronny that God is love. The words 'In our Father's house are many mansions' are adapted from the Bible (St John 14.2).

This extract is fairly typical of Forster's style in this novel. He moves from an incident in the plot, through a connected thought, to a philosophical discussion which has wide implications for the story as a whole.

6 CRITICAL APPRAISALS

For details of contemporary criticism in this section see E. M. Forster, *The Critical Heritage*, edited by Philip Gardner.

6.1 CONTEMPORARY CRITICISM

When *A Passage to India* was first published in June 1924 it was widely reviewed and generally well received. Most of the reviewers recognised that the story itself is not (and was not intended to be) the most significant aspect of the novel; they praised particularly the characterisation, the presentation of the Anglo-Indian scene, and Forster's style.

One of the first reviews was written by Rose Macaulay and published in the *Daily News* for 4 June 1924, the very day of *A Passage to India*'s publication. She grasped immediately Forster's strengths:

> His delicate character presentation...his gentle and pervading humour, his sense and conveyal of the beauty, the ridiculousness, and the nightmare strangeness, of all life, his accurate recording of social, intellectual and spiritual shades and reactions, his fine-spun honesty of thought, his poetry and ironic wit...

and concluded that it was 'the best and most interesting book' Forster had written. A little over a week later, on 14 June in the *Nation and Athenaeum*, Leonard Woolf outlined almost similar qualities and urged his readers to 'rush out to the nearest bookseller, [and] buy a copy of the book'.

Woolf's comments tempted H. W. Massingham to review the reviewers; he asserted in the *New Leader* that contemporary critics were too apt to write on literature 'as if its form-pattern, or its spiritual rhythm, and not its meaning and content, were the most important thing about it'; yet, faced with the task of isolating the 'subject' of the novel, Massingham was himself not fully confident, remarking tentatively that Forster

> . . .seems – perhaps he only seems – to suggest that if such English-men as Mr Fielding and such Englishwomen as Mrs Moore could have their say, the irreconcilable might be reconciled, the all-but-impossible accomplished.

One of the most sensitive and perceptive of the early reviewers was the novelist L. P. Hartley and it is worth quoting at length his comments on the incident in the cave and his final conclusions:

> . . .It is the central fact of the book, this gloomy expedition arranged with so much solicitude and affection by Dr. Aziz to give his guests pleasure. A lesser novelist than Mr. Forster could have shown every-thing going wrong, could have emphasized the tragic waste of Aziz's hospitality and kind intentions, could have blamed Fate. But no one else could have given the affair its peculiar horror, could have so dis-sociated it from the common course of experience and imagination, could have left it at once so vague and so clear. Unlike many cata-strophes in fiction, it seems unavoidable whichever way we look at it; we cannot belittle it by saying that the characters should have behaved more sensibly, the sun need not have been so hot or the scales weighted against happiness. And not only by the accident of the caves does Mr. Forster illustrate the incalculable disastrous fluc-tuations of human personality, but he subtly works in the black magic of India, crudely presented to us in a hundred penny-dreadfuls about the stolen eyes of idols and death-bearing charms.
>
> *A Passage to India* is a disturbing, uncomfortable book. Its surface is so delicately and finely wrought that it pricks us at a thousand points. There is no emotional repose or security about it; it is for ever puncturing our complacence, it is a bed of thorns. The humour, irony and satire that awake the attention and delight the mind on every page all leave their sting. We cannot escape to the past or the future, because Mr. Forster's method does not encourage the growth of those accretions in the mind; he pins us down to the present moment, the discontent and pain of which cannot be allayed by reference to what has been or to what will be. The action of the book is not fused by a continuous impulse; it is a series of intense isolated moments. To overstate the case very much, the characters seem with each fresh sensation to begin their lives again. And that perhaps is why no general aspect or outline of Mr. Forster's book is so satisfactory as its details.

Though the majority of the reviews which appeared immediately after the novel's publication were favourable, that of Gerald Gould in the *Saturday Review* struck a slightly sourer note. He was critical of the very qualities that most other reviewers had praised. Reading his words today we must suspect that he did not understand the novel and that he was irritated at not understanding it; this view is reinforced by his final sentence, '...all Mr Forster's dazzling and baffling wisdom leaves us only dazzled and baffled'.

There were two groups of people who might be said to have a special interest in *A Passage to India* – the Anglo-Indians and the Indians themselves. Predictably, perhaps, the Anglo-Indians felt that Forster had caricatured them. Typical of their reaction was a letter from E. A. Horne, published in the *New Statesman* for 16 August 1924. Mr Horne was generous in his appreciation of Forster's presentation of his Indian characters: 'Mr Forster has created some wonderful characters. The dear old Nawab Bahadur...the polished and charming Hamidullah; Mohammed Latif... Hassan...Aziz himself'. Even the 'English' people are

> real enough. Fielding, the author's mouthpiece; Adela, with her frank, questioning, but ever baffled nature; old Mrs Moore, with her rather shiftless, rather tiresome, mysticism, but her authentic beauty of soul.

However, he condemns utterly Forster's attempt to characterise the Anglo-Indians:

> Where have they come from? What planet do they inhabit? One rubs one's eyes. They are not even good caricatures, for an artist must see his original clearly before he can successfully caricature it. They are puppets, simulacra. The only two of them that come alive at all are Ronny, the young and rapidly becoming starched civilian, and the light-hearted Miss Derek. .... And if these people are preposterous, equally preposterous are the scenes which they enact.

The Indians, on the other hand, saw the book as a truthful reflection of the English in India. St Nihal Singh in the Calcutta *Modern Review* for September 1924 commented

> ...The plot, though quite thin, has enabled the author to accomplish two purposes. It has first of all given him the opportunity to show how the British in India despise and ostracise Indians, while on their part the Indians mistrust and misjudge the British and how the gulf between the two is widening and becoming unbridgeable. It has further given him a chance to demonstrate the utter hopelessness of expecting any improvement from the efforts of Englishmen of

superior education who arrive in India at a mature age, because they can resist the bacillus of Anglo-Indians only for a time...The author's pictures are faithful and vivid. That is particularly the case in regard to the Anglo-Indian characters he has created.

Unlike that of later Indian critics, however, Nihal Singh's stance is a slightly bitter one for he feels that, though the Anglo-Indians are accurately portrayed, the Indians themselves have been misrepresented. A more balanced view may be found in *A Survey of Anglo-Indian Fiction* by Bhupal Singh, published ten years after *A Passage to India*:

> Mr. Forster's *A Passage to India* is an oasis in the desert of Anglo-Indian fiction. It is a refreshing book, refreshing in its candour, sincerity, fairness, and art, and is worth more than the whole of the trash that passes by the name of Anglo-Indian fiction, a few writers excepted. It is a clever picture of Englishmen in India, a subtle portraiture of the Indian, especially the Moslem mind, and a fascinating study of the problems arising out of the contact of India with the West. It aims at no solution, and offers no explanation; it merely records with sincerity and insight the impressions of an English man of letters of his passage through post-War India, an Englishman who is a master of his craft, and who combines an original vision with a finished artistry. Like all original books it is intensely provoking. It does not flatter the Englishman and it does not aim at pleasing the Indian; it is likely to irritate both. It is not an imaginary picture, though it is imaginatively conceived. Most Anglo-Indian writers, as we have seen, write of India and of Indians with contempt; a very few (mostly historians) go to the other extreme. Mr. Forster's object is merely to discover how people behave in relation to one another under the conditions obtaining in India at present. That he does not win applause either from India or Anglo-India is a tribute to his impartiality.

6.2 MORE RECENT CRITICISM

During the 1930s, 1940s and 1950s a trickle of Forster criticism continued to flow but since 1960 the number of critical studies has vastly increased; practically every critic has seen *A Passage to India* as Forster's most significant work. Forster himself felt that Peter Burra's Introduction to the Everyman edition of the novel explained 'exactly' what he was trying to do and many critics have seen Lionel Trilling's 1944 study of Forster as seminal. Inevitably there has been much repetition of ideas and critical viewpoints. Here I should like to give short extracts from two more recent books, both of which seem to offer something new in their approach. Wilfred Stone is a perceptive critic of the nuances of Forster's language and style and he attempts to give a psychological interpretation of his work. John Colmer approaches Forster through the social, intellectual and cultural background of his time and offers a reinterpretation in this context.

From Wilfred Stone, *The Cave and the Mountain* (Stanford University Press, 1966), Part III, ch 12:

> Circles, containers, hollows, and swellings are, with Forster, basic symbols. His fiction is thick with dells, grottoes, hollow trees, rings, pools, rooms, houses, and in this last and greatest novel, with caves. . . .
>
> The circle has an ancient symbolic lineage. In nearly all cultures it has stood for the cyclic unity of life, the inseparability of beginning and end, the eternal round of the seasons. The wheel of life and the serpent swallowing its tail are two of man's earliest imaginings. . . [In *A Passage to India*] most important are the hollowness and roundness of the caves, and all the mythological evocations of these forms. The novel is one great echo chamber, one great round, but in so constructing it Forster is not simply creating a private fictional universe; he is re-creating the world of the Indian religious consciousness.

From John Colmer, *E. M. Forster, The Personal Voice* (Routledge & Kegan Paul, 1975) ch. 8:

> In this novel Forster makes a sharp distinction between the attempts to achieve harmony through 'completeness' and through 'reconstruction'. The former is the product of love and affection and imagination, the latter of the intellect. For the reader and for many of the characters in the novel, the people who come closest to expressing the ideal of completeness are Mrs Moore, Professor Godbole, and Dr Aziz, not so much in their ordinary everyday natures, as in the goodness of which they prove capable or which they communicate; and in the visions they enjoy. The two such dissimilar figures, Mrs Moore and Professor Godbole, provide the necessary counterweight to the vast forces of disintegration and division exerted by the chief character in the novel – India. Appropriately it is as felt presences that Forster embodies Mrs Moore and the spirit of India. But to the extent that Mrs Moore's good influence is more obviously a fictional device it may appear the weaker. It is not always noticed, however, that on her departure, Mrs Moore modifies

her nihilistic vision of India, her sense of the 'horror of the universe and its littleness'. The sight of a mosque reawakens her interest in the unknown and she longs to stop 'and disentangle the hundred Indias'. Thus, the message of the cave is not the final truth about India and she enjoys benevolent thoughts once again.

REVISION QUESTIONS

1. Examine the incident in which Aziz and Mrs Moore meet in the mosque. Discuss its significance to the novel as a whole.

2. What does Forster achieve by giving us an account of Aziz's arrest before we know what his alleged offence is?

3. Outline the part played by Mrs Moore when she is alive and discuss the significance of her influence after she is dead.

4. Show why the relationship between Fielding and Aziz breaks down. How successful is their renewed friendship at the end of the novel?

5. 'Forster poses questions but he does not answer them.' Discuss.

6. It has been suggested that Part III of *A Passage to India* is superfluous. Support or refute this suggestion.

7. Consider the significance of Forster's comments about the Indian climate in the novel.

8. Show how Forster makes use of the 'echo image' in the novel.

9. Examine in detail the last paragraph of Chapter 12 and use it as a starting point to discuss some of the ideas Forster puts forward in the novel.

10. Examine in detail the opening paragraphs of Chapter 8 (down to '...so much quarrelling and tiresomeness!') and try to suggest what light they throw on our understanding of Adela, Ronny and Mrs Moore.

FURTHER READING

Text

The Abinger Edition edited by Oliver Stallybrass (Edward Arnold, 1978) is the best text. It is reproduced, together with Stallybrass's Introduction and Notes in the Penguin Modern Classics Edition, 1979.

Other books by Forster which may help to throw further light on *A Passage to India*:

> *Where Angels Fear to Tread* (Edward Arnold, 1905).
> *The Longest Journey* (Edward Arnold, 1907).
> *Howards End* (Edward Arnold, 1910).
> *Aspects of the Novel* (Edward Arnold, 1927).
> *Abinger Harvest* (Edward Arnold, 1936).
> *The Hill of Devi* (Edward Arnold, 1953).

Also of interest are the two volumes of Forster's *Selected Letters*, eds M. Lago and P. N. Furbank (Collins, 1983-5).

Biography

The definitive biography is that by P. N. Furbank, *E. M. Forster: A Life*, 2 vols (Secker & Warburg, 1977-8).

Criticism

Colmer, John, *E. M. Forster: The Personal Voice* (Routledge & Kegan Paul, 1975).

Gardner, Philip (ed.), *E. M. Forster: The Critical Heritage* (Routledge & Kegan Paul, 1973).

Stone, Wilfred, *The Cave and the Mountain* (Stanford University Press, 1966).

Trilling, Lionel, *E. M. Forster* (Hogarth Press, 1944).

THE MACMILLAN SHAKESPEARE

General Editor: PETER HOLLINDALE
Advisory Editor: PHILIP BROCKBANK

The Macmillan Shakespeare features:
* clear and uncluttered texts with modernised punctuation and spelling wherever possible;
* full explanatory notes printed on the page facing the relevant text for ease of reference;
* stimulating introductions which concentrate on content, dramatic effect, character and imagery, rather than mere dates and sources.

Above all, The Macmillan Shakespeare treats each play as a work for the theatre which can also be enjoyed on the page.

CORIOLANUS
Editor: Tony Parr

THE WINTER'S TALE
Editor: Christopher Parry

MUCH ADO ABOUT NOTHING
Editor: Jan McKeith

RICHARD II
Editor: Richard Adams

RICHARD III
Editor: Richard Adams

HENRY IV, PART I
Editor: Peter Hollindale

HENRY IV, PART II
Editor: Tony Parr

HENRY V
Editor: Brian Phythian

AS YOU LIKE IT
Editor: Peter Hollindale

A MIDSUMMER NIGHT'S DREAM
Editor: Norman Sanders

THE MERCHANT OF VENICE
Editor: Christopher Parry

THE TAMING OF THE SHREW
Editor: Robin Hood

TWELFTH NIGHT
Editor: E. A. J. Honigmann

THE TEMPEST
Editor: A. C. Spearing

ROMEO AND JULIET
Editor: James Gibson

JULIUS CAESAR
Editor: D. R. Elloway

MACBETH
Editor: D. R. Elloway

HAMLET
Editor: Nigel Alexander

ANTONY AND CLEOPATRA
Editors: Jan McKeith and
Richard Adams

OTHELLO
Editors: Celia Hilton and R. T. Jones

KING LEAR
Editor: Philip Edwards

MACMILLAN STUDENTS' NOVELS

General Editor: JAMES GIBSON

The Macmillan Students' Novels are low-priced, new editions of major classics, aimed at the first examination candidate. Each volume contains:

* enough explanation and background material to make the novels accessible – and rewarding - to pupils with little or no previous knowledge of the author or the literary period;

* detailed notes elucidate matters of vocabulary, interpretation and historical background;

* eight pages of plates comprising facsimiles of manuscripts and early editions, portraits of the author and photographs of the geographical setting of the novels.

JANE AUSTEN: MANSFIELD PARK
Editor: Richard Wirdnam

JANE AUSTEN: NORTHANGER ABBEY
Editor: Raymond Wilson

JANE AUSTEN: PRIDE AND PREJUDICE
Editor: Raymond Wilson

JANE AUSTEN: SENSE AND SENSIBILITY
Editor: Raymond Wilson

JANE AUSTEN: PERSUASION
Editor: Richard Wirdnam

CHARLOTTE BRONTË: JANE EYRE
Editor: F. B. Pinion

EMILY BRONTË: WUTHERING HEIGHTS
Editor: Graham Handley

JOSEPH CONRAD: LORD JIM
Editor: Peter Hollindale

CHARLES DICKENS: GREAT EXPECTATIONS
Editor: James Gibson

CHARLES DICKENS: HARD TIMES
Editor: James Gibson

CHARLES DICKENS: OLIVER TWIST
Editor: Guy Williams

CHARLES DICKENS: A TALE OF TWO CITIES
Editor: James Gibson

GEORGE ELIOT: SILAS MARNER
Editor: Norman Howlings

GEORGE ELIOT: THE MILL ON THE FLOSS
Editor: Graham Handley

D. H. LAWRENCE: SONS AND LOVERS
Editor: James Gibson

D. H. LAWRENCE: THE RAINBOW
Editor: James Gibson

MARK TWAIN: HUCKLEBERRY FINN
Editor: Christopher Parry

Mastering English Language
Richard Gill

Mastering English Literature will help readers both to enjoy English Literature and to be successful in 'O' levels, 'A' levels and other public exams. It is an introduction to the study of poetry, novels and drama which helps the reader in four ways – by providing ways of approaching literature, by giving examples and practice exercises, by offering hints on how to write about literature, and by the author's own evident enthusiasm for the subject. With extracts from more than 200 texts, this is an enjoyable account of how to get the maximum satisfaction out of reading, whether it be for formal examinations or simply for pleasure.

Work Out English Language ('A' level)
S.H. Burton

This book familiarises 'A' level English Literature candidates with every kind of test which they are likely to encounter. Suggested answers are worked out step by step and accompanied by full author's commentary. The book helps students to clarify their aims and establish techniques and standards so that they can make appropriate responses to similar questions when the examination pressures are on. It opens up fresh ways of looking at the full range of set texts, authors and critical judgements and motivates students to know more of these matters.